Fake News in the Gospel

Trilogy by Joseph Codsi

1 – The Christian Fable

Inspired by *The Mystic Fable* by Michel de Certeau.

2 – Enigmatic Texts in the Gospel and the Constitution

An enigmatic text "does not mention what it knows; it hides what organizes it; it unveils solely by its form what it erases from its content."

3 – Fake News in the Gospel

Jesus was guilty as charged;
therefore, he was not the innocent Lamb of God whose death redeemed the world.

His resurrection, on the other hand, is based on pious illusions.

*

Fake News
in the
GOSPEL

Jesus Was Guilty as Charged

JOSEPH CODSI

RESOURCE *Publications* • Eugene, Oregon

FAKE NEWS IN THE GOSPEL
Jesus Was Guilty as Charged

Copyright © 2024 Joseph Codsi. All rights reserved. Except for brief quotations in critical publications or reviews, no part of this book may be reproduced in any manner without prior written permission from the publisher. Write: Permissions, Wipf and Stock Publishers, 199 W. 8th Ave., Suite 3, Eugene, OR 97401.

Resource Publications
An Imprint of Wipf and Stock Publishers
199 W. 8th Ave., Suite 3
Eugene, OR 97401

www.wipfandstock.com

PAPERBACK ISBN: 978-1-6667-8889-1
HARDCOVER ISBN: 978-1-6667-8890-7
EBOOK ISBN: 978-1-6667-8891-4

VERSION NUMBER 041624

All scripture quotations are taken from the *Open English Bible*.

I reproduce, in this book, many ideas that can be found in the first part of my previous book, *Enigmatic Texts in the Gospel and the Constitution*.

*

Because I was a Jew, I found myself free from many prejudices that limited others in the use of their intellect; and, being a Jew, I was prepared to enter opposition and to renounce agreement with the 'compact majority'.

—Sigmund Freud[1]

*

People of faith need theology—good, sound, robust theology. You've probably heard the saying that goes "bad company corrupts good character." Bad theology corrupts, well, everything.

—Emily Lund[2]

*

I used to think that way when I was studying for the priesthood.
Now I have become less naïve.
I think that theology is the study of pious dreams
that are mistaken for revealed Truth.
I am not a gospel scholar. Therefore, I do not follow the historical-critical method that gospel scholars must follow.
What Freud discovered about repressed memories and the return of the repressed is of great value for the interpretation of three enigmatic texts that are found in the Gospel of Mark.
The text resists those who make it say what it does not say, as well as those who do not see what is in it.

—Joseph Codsi

---

1. Letter to the B'nai B'rith Lodge of Vienna, which in 1926 celebrated his seventieth birthday.

2. Tyler Hansen and Emily Lund, *Napkin Theology, Small Drawings about Big Ideas*, illustrated by Jodie Londono. Cascade Books, Eugene, Oregon. 2003. XV.

The theological and exegetical worlds do not need to be shaken to their foundations: they need to be utterly and thoroughly demolished and rebuilt from the bottom up. The way scholars have engaged the biblical text for the past 200 or so years has gotten us virtually nowhere. Fad methodologies have come and gone, and we still can't assert with any sense of assurance that 'this biblical passage means this' (indeed many would suggest these days that texts don't mean anything, it is only what the reader thinks that matters).

—Jim West[3]

*

Gospel scholars seem to have exhausted the study of our sacred texts. This pushes their research toward external evidence. What they cannot find in the text, they look for it outside the text.
My study is a return to the text, which is justified, because I have discovered new evidence in the text.
It is hard to believe that crucial information exists in the gospels of Mark and John that has remained unknown to this day. This makes my discovery as important as what Galileo and Darwin discovered in their respective fields.

*

Many have contested the claims of the Christian religion concerning Jesus Christ, Son of God. They relied on external evidence. I do the same thing, but I rely on internal evidence that is found hidden in the text of the gospel.

J.C.

*

---

3. Foreword to *Mimetic Criticism and the Gospel of Mark*, by Joel L. Watts, Wipf and Stock, Eugene, Oregon. 2013. IX.

The Christian Religion
is based on
a pious illusion,
the resurrection
of Jesus.

*

If Jesus Christ has not been raised,
your faith is worthless.

Paul in 1 Corinthians 15:17

Contents

My Prejudiced Ideas | xi
Etymology of the word "gospel" | xiii
Historicity Criterion | xv
Warning | xvii

Raw Ideas | 1
The two parts of this book | 9

Part One—**What happened after the death of Jesus** | 15
Chapter 1—Two Burial Stories in the Gospel of John | 17
Chapter 2—A Spiritual Understanding of the Resurrection in the Gospel of John | 32
Chapter 3—Apparitions' Stories | 41

Part Two—**What happened during the life of Jesus.** | 51
Chapter 1—Repressed Memoriesin the Gospel of Mark | 53
Chapter 2—Other manifestations of the dualism between pre- and post-Pascal in Mark's narrative | 101

Appendix 1—Note on the Eucharist | 133
Appendix 2—The Beloved Disciple | 138

Bibliography | 153
About the Author | 155

My Prejudiced Ideas

The testimony of Peter,
as it is reproduced in the Gospel of Mark,
reveals a deeply disturbed mind.

He identifies with the demons
who proclaim that Jesus is the Messiah
in flagrant disobedience to his stern orders not to do so.

*

Etymology of the word "gospel"

The word 'gospel" means "good news." It comes from old English and it combines two words, "gōd" and "spel." *Gōd* means 'good' and *spel* means 'news.'

The Greek word *'evangelion'* that means 'gospel' is structured in a similar way. It consists of two parts, a prefix 'ev' that means 'good' and a word *'angelion'* that means 'news.' The word *'angel'* comes from the same root and means *'messenger.'*

*

Another formulation of my title
can be
Fake News
in the
Good News

*

Fake News in the Gospel

I claim that
the Christian religion is based
on pious but fake news
that systematically transformed what happened during the life of Jesus
in order to show that he knew about God's plan concerning his death and resurrection.

*

Is fake news what Jesus allegedly said before the High Priest during his trial
that justified his condemnation to death.

In reality, Jesus' condemnation was perfectly justified.
He was condemned as a dangerous lunatic who claims to have received divine revelations that were radically incompatible with traditional Judaism.
Those revelations did not concern his identity as Messiah and Son of God,
but the Temple and its sacrifices.

*

Historicity Criterion

Is pre-Pascal what happened during the life of Jesus up to his death.

Is post-Pascal what happened after the death of Jesus, namely his resurrection and deification.

During his life, nobody including Jesus himself knew anything about what was going to happen after his death.

Therefore,

is not historical
whatever anticipates the Pascal revelation
in pre-Pascal time.

No other historicity criterion is needed.

This is so, because the disciples and eyewitnesses of what happened during the life of Jesus had one big problem, how to reconcile what happened during the life of Jesus that ended in a big failure with their Easter or Pascal faith in the resurrection that most radically transformed Jesus in their eyes.

*

Warning

This book's conclusions are based on a meticulous reading of the Gospels of John and Mark.

It is true that all our four gospels proclaim the Christian faith in Jesus as Christ and Son of God, whose sacrificial death on the cross redeemed the world. But this is a superficial and naïve reading of our sacred texts.

Gospel scholarship, on the other hand, is less naïve. It can be described as a critical reading of the gospel. But, so far, it has followed the historical-critical method which relies on what the text says overtly. It ignores what the text says covertly. My methodology is more advanced. It allows me to spot what is only implied in the text and memories that were repressed.

As far as I am concerned, my study of the gospel is as revolutionary as Galileo's discovery that the earth is not the immobile center of the world, or Darwin's discovery of evolution. This will undoubtedly sound very arrogant. But I'll let you be my judge, since you have started reading my book. No previous knowledge of the gospel is required.

This book is not for pious Christians

The Christian religion, like all other religions, is not based on verifiable knowledge, but on respectable spiritual experiences that have engendered highly sophisticated theological discourses. Religions answer some basic human needs. But they are based on naïve interpretations of what is "revealed" in dreams and visions. What is so revealed comes from the subconscious activity of the brain. This activity is perceived as coming from another world. I think that what pertains to this world and the other world is based on the dual activity of the brain that can be identified as conscious and subconscious. Conscious activity produces science, which is based on verifiable knowledge. The subconscious activity produces mythical feelings.

*

Raw Ideas

*

Jesus was a Jewish prophet.
In the last phase of his life,
he received new revelations concerning God's plans for Israel.

In the end times, he proclaimed,
there will be no need for sacrificial offerings.
The Temple and its sacrifices will become obsolete,
and the Passover meal will be celebrated anywhere in the world,
not just in Jerusalem.[1]

When he revealed this in Galilee to the five and four thousand
people who had come to listen to him,
they recognized in him a new Moses
and wanted to make him king.
But he rejected the idea and lost his popularity.
When he repeated the same declaration in the Temple,
he was arrested, tried and condemned to death.

---

1. After the Romans destroyed Jerusalem and the Temple, the Temple sacrifices stopped. The Passover meal ritual had to be adjusted to this new reality. Some Christians saw a vindication of Jesus in this calamity. I think that we have no way of knowing anything about questions of this kind. What the Romans did had nothing to do with what Jesus thought or said. Besides, what he might have said on this topic is likely to have been distorted in the Christian memory.

Fake News in the Gospel

This would have been the end of his story
were it not for the disciples' resurrection experience.
They believed that God had resurrected him
and elevated him to the divine realm.
They made him Christ and Son of God after his death,
in spite of his violent opposition to such nonsense during his life.

*

The Christian religion is based on a pious illusion
that caused the disciples to believe in the resurrection of Jesus.
Under the influence of this faith they were forced to manipulate many facts.
On one hand, they invented stories that confirmed their faith,
but, on the other hand, they repressed the memories of very important events
that would have rendered their Christian faith untenable.
Thus, they have falsely reported that when Jesus was alive he had recognized that he was the Messiah, but they claimed that he wanted to keep this identity secret before the resurrection.

In reality, Jesus' message was not about him but about God.
He rejected the Messianic crown, because he had never thought of himself as a Messiah, and because this idea was incompatible with his message.

But after his death and their resurrection experience, the disciples became convinced that God had elevated him to the rank of Messiah and Son of God.

In order to resolve the conflict between Jesus' rejection of the Messianic crown and what was revealed to them after his death, they invented the notion that his rejection of the Messianic crown was only temporary.
This is how they rationalized their way around the problem.
And this is what we find in the Gospel of Mark.

*

This kind of manipulation of the facts could not have been done
by second generation believers
such as the gospel writers.
Only those who knew what took place during the life of Jesus
could have done so
once they had become witnesses to the resurrection.
One exception existed, however,
this was Judas Iscariot.
He was demonized, most likely, because he could not believe in
the resurrection
and refused to be part of the reprehensible manipulation of many
important events that
had to be either transformed or repressed or invented
with the sole purpose of making the faith in the resurrection
possible.

*

Gospel scholars distinguish between the historical Jesus and the
Christ of the faith.
The historical Jesus was only a messenger of what was revealed to
him.
The Christ of the faith became the central message of the
Apostles.
Freud made a similar but different distinction.
He said that Judaism is a religion of the Father, and Christianity a
religion of the Son.
In reality, the religion of Jesus was a religion of the Father.
The disciples invented the religion of the Son and combined it
with the religion of the Father.

Jesus did not intend to start a new religion;
he just wanted to reform Judaism
based on the revelations that he had received.

*

Fake News in the Gospel

I claim that the disciples of Jesus
(all eleven of them, not counting Judas,
or just a few of them including Peter,
the source of Mark's information)
had severe mental problems once they had become
witnesses to the resurrection.

Their resurrection experience was real, not fake.
It affected them deeply.
But it did not affect the dead body of Jesus.
To overcome this formidable problem
they invented the two stories of the empty tomb and of Jesus'
burial by Joseph of Arimathea.

The gospels of Mark and John confirm in their different ways
all the wild statements that I have made so far.

*

Baptism

People become Christian through baptism. So did Jesus. He was baptized twice. The first time, he went to the Jordan River, to the spot where John was baptizing. That was a pre-Christian baptism. John baptized people for the forgiveness of their sins. Jesus was baptized a second time. This was when he died and was resurrected.

In the Christian baptism those two components are united. One is submerged into water, which is an act of drowning and symbolizes death, then one emerges from the water, which symbolizes return to life and resurrection. In Jesus' case, his death was not symbolic; it was real.

Note. In Mark 10:35 the death of Jesus is identified as baptism.

*

In his famous letters, Paul explains this association between baptism and the death of Christ. He also explains why the resurrection of Jesus is so central to the Christian faith. If Jesus was not raised from the dead, he wrote, then the entire Christian religion would fall apart.

As far as the Christian faith is concerned, the resurrection of Jesus was an act of God. But we can raise the question, "What if the resurrection was an act of the disciples?" If we can show that this was the case, then it will become evident that the entire Christian religion is based on a pious illusion.

There is no doubt that the disciples' resurrection experience was genuine. They did go through powerful mystical experiences in which they saw the resurrected Christ and interacted with him. But it is quite possible that this spiritual experience did not affect the dead body of Jesus. To link their spiritual experience to the body of Jesus, they invented the empty-tomb story. Now, if we can show that the empty-tomb story is a pious invention of the disciples, then the entire Christian faith falls apart.

This is not all. The disciples of Jesus became pathological liars after their resurrection experience. They had to hide very important actions of Jesus that would have rendered their Christian faith in him, as Messiah and Son of God, impossible.

Only a meticulous study of Mark's Gospel can show that my theory is correct. Mark's narrative consists of two discourses, one that is overt and another one that is covert. The overt discourse is based on the way the disciples of Jesus told his story after his death and after they had gone through their resurrection experience. The covert discourse reveals that their memory of what Jesus had said and done was altered under the influence of their resurrection experience.

The covert discourse has remained unrecognized to this day. Its main feature is that it reveals important things that did take place during the life of Jesus but had to be repressed, because they contradicted the Easter faith of the disciples.

*

Raw Ideas

History and Theology

In the Christian religion history and theology are inseparable. History says what happened during the life of Jesus up to his death. Theology says the place of Jesus in the divine plan.

The divine plan was formulated in two stages. The first stage is ascending. It goes up from earth to heaven. The second phase is descending. It comes down from heaven to earth. The first stage was revealed first. It is based on the resurrection of Jesus and his elevation to heaven, the divine realm. In this first stage Jesus was deified. According to the second stage, the Son of God was made man and was born from a virgin. This second phase is known as Incarnation (God becoming physically human). The second stage appears in the Gospels of Matthew and Luke, which tell how the Virgin Mary gave birth to Jesus. In its prologue, the Gospel of John speaks of the Incarnation in more abstract terms. It states that the Divine Logos[2] became human flesh and dwelled among us.

The second stage is entirely theological. It is not based on anything that the disciples of Jesus could have witnessed. I will not be concerned with it in this study.

The first stage, on the other hand, is crucial. It is entirely based on the resurrection experience of the disciples. That experience deified him in their minds.

*

So far, I have put my ideas on the table. Now you know what I think. This is the easy part. In what follows, I must explain how and why I have come to those conclusions. This is the hard part for me as well as for you. I invite you to read my book critically. But, to do so, you must understand what I am saying and why I am saying it. This will require a lot of effort and concentration from you. Please take your time. This is not a novel that can be read in one session. Make sure you understand the logic that guides me. If need be, read the same section twice. If you have questions, don't

---

2. The spoken Word of God.

hesitate to email me at josephcodsi@hotmail.com. I have done most of my work; yours is just beginning.

The two parts of this book

In the first part, I will discuss the resurrection experience of the disciples. This was a real and powerful experience, but it did not affect the dead body of Jesus.

In the second part, I will show how the disciples' memory of what Jesus did and said during his life was altered in order to hide some memories that contradicted their Christian faith and replace them with fake memories that confirmed their faith in the resurrected Christ.

In other words, Jesus was not the founder of the Christian religion. The disciples were. Their resurrection experience revealed to them the theological dimension of Jesus. They transformed the historical Jesus accordingly. Thus, their eyewitness testimony of what happened during the life of Jesus was systematically tainted by their theological faith in Jesus Christ, Son of God, whose death was sacrificial and redemptive. The historical Jesus knew nothing of that theological understanding.

*

1—What happened after the death of Jesus

The disciples of Jesus had an extraordinary experience. They became convinced that God had resurrected Jesus. This was a real and powerful experience. It transformed Jesus from a failed prophet to a triumphant Lord and Christ. The faith in the resurrection was going to deify him in the eyes of the Christian world. It did transform the disciples as well. They became witnesses to the resurrection, and they were ready to die for that faith.

But from the very beginning their faith in the resurrection was on shaky ground. Even if their resurrection experience was real, this does not mean that it did affect the dead body of Jesus. In other words, the body of Jesus could have remained in the grave, while he appeared to them in a dream-like mystical experience. This is why they had to show that the dead body of Jesus was no longer in the tomb. To do so, they invented the story of Joseph of Arimathea, the good Samaritan who gave Jesus an honorable burial in an easily identifiable tomb, while the female disciples of Jesus observed what he did. This made it possible for the female disciples to discover the empty tomb on the first day of the week.

I discuss this question in a chapter entitled, "Two Burial Stories in the Gospel of John."

In a second chapter, I discuss a special understanding of the resurrection that is found in the long farewell speech in the Gospel of John. In it the author explains why the resurrected Jesus appeared only to his disciples and not to anybody else. His explanation is that only those who miss Jesus dearly after his death have the privilege of seeing him. In this discussion, psychological considerations are introduced. This acknowledges the spiritual and subjective nature of the resurrection experience.

In a third chapter, I go over the apparitions' stories and what they reveal about the disciples' experience.

*

2—What happened during the life of Jesus

This second part will be quite different from the first one. The first one is based on what the gospels say overtly. The second part is based on what the gospel of Mark says covertly. Because what is said there has remained unrecognized to this day, we will discover new things in Mark's narrative. When Jesus was at the height of

The two parts of this book

his popularity in Galilee, he received new revelations concerning God's plans for Israel. He believed that a new phase in Israel's history will open. The Temple sacrifices will become obsolete, and Passover will be celebrated anywhere in the world as a non-sacrificial meal.

When Jesus proclaimed this new revelation to the five and four thousand people who had come to listen to him, they recognized in him a new Moses and wanted to make him king. But he rejected the idea and lost his popularity. He was left with the twelve disciples and a few women. From then on, he had to act alone, go up to Jerusalem and proclaim in the Temple what he had proclaimed in Galilee. He was arrested on the spot, tried, and crucified as a dangerous lunatic.

But everything changed when the disciples became witnesses to the resurrection. They became convinced that God had resurrected his servant Jesus and elevated him to heaven. This Easter or Pascal faith became their unshakable truth. Everything else had to be subordinated to it. Consequently, they repressed all memories that contradicted their Easter faith. But the memories that were repressed returned in disguise. The disguise took the form of enigmatic texts that made no sense. A new interpretation of those texts shows that the disciples tampered with the evidence. They suppressed any evidence that could have rendered their faith in the resurrection unsustainable. And they did so under duress. A mysterious force made them do so. This is where Freud's discovery of repressed memories and the return of the repressed allows us to reconstruct what must have happened with a great deal of certainty.

*

The death of Jesus is the dividing line between "before" and "after." What happened after his death is centered on the resurrection experience of the disciples. What happened before his death is not easy to reconstruct. It is based on the memory of the disciples and eyewitnesses. But there are reasons to believe that their memory was altered under the powerful influence of their resurrection experience. A new methodology is going to be needed to identify the mental processes that caused them to repress important memories and invent pious stories that confirmed their faith in Jesus Christ, Son of God.

Luke recognizes the central role of the disciples in the transmission of what we know about Jesus.

> [1]Many attempts have been already made to write an account of those events which have taken place among us, [2]just as they were reported to us by those who from the beginning were eyewitnesses, and afterward became bearers of the message. [3]And, therefore, I also, since I have investigated all these events with great care from their very beginning, have resolved to write an orderly account of them for you, [4]in order that you may be able to satisfy yourself of the accuracy of the story which you have heard from the lips of others.
> Luke 1:1–4

What Luke is emphasizing here is our reliance on the disciples of Jesus. He assumed as all Christians do that what we know about Jesus is based on their testimony and that they were highly dependable witnesses of what happened during the life of Jesus. This is what I am contesting in this book. I claim that the disciples and eyewitnesses were highly unreliable, simply because they had to distort many things that had taken place during the life of Jesus that would have rendered their faith in Jesus Christ, Son of God, baseless.

I am interested here in the logic of the faith, as Luke understood it, not in what some gospel scholars might think as historians. Many of them think, as historians, that what we have in our four canonical gospels is not based on eyewitness testimony. I agree with them that none of the gospel writers were eyewitnesses of what happened during the life of Jesus. But I think that Papias was correct when he said that Mark's gospel is based on what he heard Peter say about Jesus. This connection, when it is recognized, can

The two parts of this book

change radically the way we read and interpret the Gospel of Mark. This is what is new and revolutionary in this book.

I think that, in his introduction to the gospel, Luke recognizes the two functions that the disciples fulfilled. The first one is the most obvious one. They were eyewitnesses of what happened during the life of Jesus. The second one is alluded to as their being "servants of the word." As servants of the word, they proclaimed the Christian faith in Jesus Christ, Son of God. They acted as witnesses to the resurrection. Luke does not see any conflict between these two functions. I disagree with him. I think that the disciples had to serve two masters, History and Theology. They betrayed History so that they could remain true to Theology. They transformed the past by omission and by addition. For instance, they omitted to mention the real reason why Jesus was condemned to death. If they recognized that he was guilty as charged, he could not be the innocent Lamb of God whose sacrificial death saved the world. Quite logically they could not recognize that Jesus was guilty as charged and that his death sentence was justified. They projected, on the other hand, the image of the resurrected Christ back onto the historical Jesus. They claimed that Jesus was the Messiah during his life, but that he wanted to keep his Messianic identity secret before the resurrection.

We have here two understandings of the Christian event that cannot be reconciled. The overt discourse of the four canonical gospels agrees with Luke and confirms the traditional faith. But there is, in the Gospel of Mark a covert discourse that agrees with me. That covert discourse has remained unrecognized to this day.

*

PART ONE

What happened after the death of Jesus

*

After his death, Jesus was buried. Nothing else happened to him. But formidable things happened to his disciples. They became witnesses to his resurrection, and they felt empowered to proclaim the good news of their gospel.

Gospel scholars form two groups. One group believes in the physical resurrection of Jesus. That group is theologically correct. The other group thinks that the faith in the resurrection of Jesus was based on a spiritual experience that affected the disciples without affecting the dead body of Jesus. Theologically speaking, this second view is incorrect. I will show that, although this view is theologically incorrect, it is historically correct.

In a book entitled "Jesus' Resurrection: Fact or Figment?" a debate is reproduced that opposed William Lane Craig and Gerd Lüdemann. The debate took place at Boston College. For Craig, the resurrection affected not only the disciples, but also the body of Jesus. Lüdemann, on the other hand, defended the other alternative. For him the resurrection affected the disciples, not the body

Part One—What happened after the death of Jesus

of Jesus. Craig made two important points. All four gospels reproduce the burial by Joseph of Arimathea and the empty-tomb story. Therefore, he concluded, they must be historical. The second point is that there is no other burial story that we know of. Lüdemann had no way of showing that the burial by Joseph of Arimathea was fake news. Also, he did not know that another burial story existed in the Gospel of John. Consequently, he failed to defend his thesis.

In the following chapter, I will show that the story of the burial by Joseph of Arimathea was forged, and that there is in the Gospel of John a story that implies that the Roman soldiers buried Jesus.

I will introduce, on the other hand, some new knowledge that is based on a study of the mystical experience by Michel de Certeau. We shall see that the resurrection experience of the disciples has a lot in common with the mystical experience. Certeau published a book entitled "*The Mystic Fable.*" As the title suggests, the mystics go through dreams and visions that are as true as fables. A fable is a story that conveys some meaning or wisdom but is, by definition, fiction. It can be compared to a parable. In the last analysis, what the mystics believe to be revelations from the other world is the product of their subconscious.

*

Chapter 1

Two Burial Stories in the Gospel of John[1]

"The distortion of a text is not unlike a murder.
The difficulty lies not in the execution of the deed
but in the doing away with the traces."[2]

The two burial stories appear side by side in John's narrative.

First burial story

A [31]It was Preparation Day, and so, to prevent the bodies from remaining on the crosses during the Sabbath (for that Sabbath was a great day), the Jews asked Pilate to have the legs broken and the bodies removed. [32]Accordingly the soldiers came and broke the legs of the first man, and then those of the other who had been crucified with Jesus; [33]but, on coming to him,

---

1. This paper was published in *The Fourth R*, November-December 2018.
2. Sigmund Freud, *Moses and Monotheism*, translated by Katherine Jones (Hogarth Press and the Institute of Psychoanalysis, 1939) 70. A PDF copy of the book is now available on the Internet.

Part One—What happened after the death of Jesus

when they saw that he was already dead, they did not break his legs.

B ³⁴One of the soldiers, however, pierced his side with a spear, and blood and water immediately flowed from it. ³⁵This is the statement of one who actually saw it—and his statement may be relied on, and he knows that he is speaking the truth—and it is given in order that you also may be convinced. ³⁶For all this happened in fulfillment of the words of scripture—'Not one of its bones will be broken.' ³⁷And there is another passage which says—'They will look on him whom they pierced.'

John 19:31–37

Second burial story

³⁸After this, Joseph of Arimathea, a disciple of Jesus—but a secret one, owing to his fear of the religious authorities—begged Pilate's permission to remove the body of Jesus. Pilate gave him leave; so Joseph went and removed the body. ³⁹Nicodemus, too—the man who had formerly visited Jesus by night—came with a roll of myrrh and aloes, weighing nearly a hundred pounds. ⁴⁰They took the body of Jesus, and wound it in linen with the spices, according to the Jewish mode of burial. ⁴¹At the place where Jesus had been crucified there was a garden, and in the garden a newly made tomb in which no one had ever been laid. ⁴²And so, because of its being the Preparation Day, and as the tomb was close at hand, they laid Jesus there.

John 19:38–42

First story

I have divided the first story into two parts. Part A reports what was in the source used by John. Part B introduces new concerns that are unique to John. In itself, Part A is of no interest to John.

He uses it only to explain why the soldiers did not break the legs of Jesus, which is for him a sign that Jesus is the Passover lamb of which no bone can be broken. In other words, John's primary concern was theological not historical.

Next comes the piercing of Jesus' side (Part B) and the coming out of blood and water. This is the point that is of interest to John, who sees in it a miraculous sign that calls for faith. This sign is strengthened by the fulfillment of two scriptures.

Verse 35 is in the center of Part B. It introduces the witness who saw what the soldiers did and what happened when one of them pierced the side of Jesus with his lance. Now this witness remains a mystery. Who was he? The Greek text refers to him in the masculine form. So, he must be one of the male disciples. But according to Mark 15:50, all the male disciples of Jesus ran away when he was arrested. Only some female disciples were present near the crucifixion place. According to John, however, the disciple whom Jesus loved was present there with Mary, the mother of Jesus (see John 19:25–27). The Beloved Disciple is mentioned only in the Gospel of John and his identity remains a mystery. I have written a paper about him. You can find it in Appendix 2. Let me say here that what pertains to the Beloved Disciple is likely to involve special theological insights that are unique to John and his gospel.

This explains why John forgets so easily the last part of what the soldiers had done, namely that they removed the bodies of the three crucified men once they were dead and disposed of them in a common grave. None of the disciples, including the women, knew where it was. The women could have seen the soldiers come and break the legs of the two men who were crucified along with Jesus. But as the sun was about to set, they had to leave on account of the Sabbath. They did not see the soldiers remove the bodies and do what they had to do.

John left the action of the soldiers unfinished. But they must have obeyed the orders they had received and made sure no traces of the crucifixion were left during the Sabbath. John reported what

Part One—What happened after the death of Jesus

the soldiers were ordered to do, because this was for him a way of introducing an important testimony of the Beloved Disciple.

*

Second story

The second story is centered on Joseph of Arimathea, who went to see Pilate and asked permission "to let him remove the body of Jesus." His obvious intention was to give Jesus an honorable burial. His request differs from that of the Jewish council in one major point: he was interested only in Jesus. He had no objection to leaving the other two men on the crosses during the Sabbath. In other words, Joseph did not share the concern of the Jewish leadership to have the crucifixion ordeal ended before a particularly important day.

The second story is well known. Not only is it found in John, but it is also the only burial story in Mark, Matthew, and Luke. In comparison, the first burial story is barely implied in the text of John. This is why, I suppose, it has been ignored to this day.

I will argue that the second burial story was derived from the first one. But first, I would like to analyze the significant discrepancies that plague the four accounts of the second story. They show that each evangelist tried to overcome the problems inherent in that second story.

*

Two Burial Stories in the Gospel of John

Part 1—Comparative study of the second burial's four versions

We have read John's version. Here are the others.

Mark

⁴²The evening had already fallen, when, as it was Preparation Day—the day before the Sabbath—⁴³Joseph from Arimathea, a councilor of good position, who was himself living in expectation of the kingdom of God, came and ventured to go in to see Pilate, and to ask for the body of Jesus. ⁴⁴But Pilate was surprised to hear that he had already died. So he sent for the officer, and asked if he was already dead; ⁴⁵and, on learning from the officer that it was so, he gave the corpse to Joseph. ⁴⁶Joseph, having bought a linen sheet, took Jesus down, and wound the sheet around him, and laid him in a tomb which had been cut out of the rock; and then rolled a stone up against the entrance of the tomb. ⁴⁷Mary of Magdala and Mary, the mother of Joseph, were watching to see where he was laid.

Mark 15:42–47

Matthew

⁵⁷When evening had fallen, there came a rich man from Arimathea, named Joseph, who had himself become a disciple of Jesus. ⁵⁸He went to see Pilate, and asked for the body of Jesus. Pilate ordered it to be given him. ⁵⁹So Joseph took the body, and wrapped it in a clean linen sheet, ⁶⁰and laid it in his newly made tomb which he had cut in the rock; and, before he left, he rolled a great stone against the entrance of the tomb. ⁶¹Mary of Magdala and the other Mary remained behind, sitting in front of the grave.

Matt 27:57–61

Part One—What happened after the death of Jesus

Luke

⁵⁰Now there was a man of the name of Joseph, who was a member of the Council, and who bore a good and upright character. ⁵¹(This man had not assented to the decision and action of the Council.) He belonged to Arimathea, a town in Judea, and lived in expectation of the kingdom of God. ⁵²He now went to see Pilate, and asked for the body of Jesus; ⁵³and, when he had taken it down, he wrapped it in a linen sheet, and laid him in a tomb cut out of stone, in which no one had yet been buried. ⁵⁴It was Preparation Day, and just before the Sabbath began. ⁵⁵The women who had accompanied Jesus from Galilee followed, and saw the tomb and how the body of Jesus was laid, ⁵⁶and then went home, and prepared spices and perfumes.

Luke 23:50–55

Main differences

The three synoptic gospels make sure that the women knew where the body of Jesus was laid. This was essential for the story of the empty tomb, in which it is assumed that the women had witnessed what Joseph of Arimathea had done. Only John fails to mention this point. He has Mary Magdalene go to the tomb early on the first day of the week[3]. How did she identify the tomb? This inconsistency suggests that John picked up the story, from Mark or its source, in which the women see where Joseph of Arimathea had left the corpse of Jesus. According to Mark, Jesus was hastily buried, and the ritual preparation of the body was not performed but rather was left for the women to do after the Sabbath[4]. John realized that putting the ritual off until then meant that Jesus had not received a proper burial, so he had Joseph and Nicodemus perform the ritual burial and, I should add, without the presence of the women. In addition, John must have

---

3. See John 20:1
4. See Mark 16:1.

thought that Joseph could not handle burying Jesus all by himself, so he gave him Nicodemus as a helper.

The time factor

Mark states that Joseph went to see Pilate "when evening had come." This means that, if Joseph was concerned with observing the Sabbath law, he had to act quickly because the interval between evening and night is short in that part of the world. Matthew paid special attention to this point. He reduced Joseph's activity to the bare minimum: wrapping the body in a clean linen cloth and depositing it in his own tomb. Thus, Joseph did not have to go and buy anything for the burial of Jesus, as in Mark (and John), and he did not have to look for a tomb, as in John.

John, on the other hand, does not mention that evening had come when Joseph went to see Pilate. This provided more time for what Joseph (and Nicodemus) had to do. In John's story, Nicodemus comes with a wagonload of myrrh and aloes, and the two good Samaritans gave Jesus a royal burial, a time-consuming activity. But, at the end, they had to hurry and find a tomb, because the day of Preparation was about to end and the Sabbath about to start. So, they just used a tomb that was there! John's story is not realistic here. Matthew is the only one who cared to avoid the strange conduct of using a tomb that was just there.

*

The identity of Joseph of Arimathea

According to Mark, Joseph was member of the Jewish council. This identification was problematic because the council had handed Jesus over to Pilate for crucifixion. Mark emphasizes that the council's verdict was unanimous (Mark 14:64), which obviously implies that Joseph had voted to condemn Jesus—an embarrassing problem that Luke explicitly contradicts in Luke 24:51. In order

Part One—What happened after the death of Jesus

to overcome this difficulty, Mark specified that Joseph was a pious Jew who waited expectantly for the Kingdom of God (Mark 15:43). Matthew must have thought that piety was not enough to motivate Joseph's action. He transformed him into a disciple of Jesus. He also made him a rich man in order to explain how he could afford to have his own tomb hewn out in the rock.

In order to make Joseph's action believable, Mark spoke of the courage he showed when he "boldly" went to Pilate to request the body of Jesus. Matthew and Luke omit this detail.

John avoided a big problem by not associating Joseph with the council. For him, Joseph was a secret disciple of Jesus. This explains his concern about Jesus, but not the access he had to Pilate. If he was not an important person, he would not have had a chance to reach the Roman governor.[5] This is a weak point in John's story. But he was wise to give Joseph a helper in the person of Nicodemus.

Conclusion

This quick survey of the four accounts shows that the tradition of a burial by Joseph of Arimathea was problematic. Each gospel writer tried to fix it as best as they could.

In all four narratives, Joseph of Arimathea appears out of the blue and saves the day. Not only does he give Jesus an honorable burial, but he provides the premise for the empty tomb story. This is why he reminds me of a *deus ex machina*, lowered in a basket at the end of a Greek play, who resolves all the problems.

As a *deus ex machina* Joseph appears to be fictive, and the four gospel accounts concerning what he did for Jesus are likely to be pious fictions as well. But is the evidence really conclusive? I must admit that all the evidence that I have produced so far is circumstantial. An impartial jury might find it impressive, but

---

5. John was perceptive enough to give Peter an associate who could help him gain access to the high priest's courtyard (see John 18:15–16). He should have known that, as disciple of Jesus, Joseph could not have had access to Pilate.

not conclusive. Is it possible to produce some really compelling evidence?

*

Part 2—How the second burial story evolved from the first one

The proof that Joseph's story is a pious fiction can be found in Mark's text. Let us read it once more.

> [42]The evening had already fallen, when, as it was Preparation Day—the day before the Sabbath—[43]Joseph from Arimathea, a councilor of good position, who was himself living in expectation of the kingdom of God, came and ventured to go in to see Pilate, and to ask for the body of Jesus.
> Mark 15:42–43

There is, in this text, a causal connection between Joseph's request and the fact that "it was the day of Preparation." This is very strange, because the impending sabbath had nothing to do with Joseph's request. He just wanted to give Jesus an honorable burial. He was not concerned about the two other men who were crucified with Jesus. As far as he was concerned, they could have remained crucified during the coming holy day. If he had acted in anticipation of the impending holy day, he would have included the two other men in his request. What seems to have happened is that Mark (or more likely the tradition he is following) transformed the story of the first burial using a simple substitution: the original request from the Jewish leadership became a request from just one of them, Joseph of Arimathea. In the first story, it is the impending holy day that motivated "the Jews" to request the removal of the bodies. But it is clear that Joseph was not interested in all three men, only in Jesus. Mark has inadvertently reproduced a feature of the first burial story in his new version. While the explanation, "since it was the day of Preparation," made sense in the first story, it did not in the second one. Matthew and Luke removed that incoherent reference to the day of Preparation. Mark's mistake is the "smoking gun" that shows that he knew the first story when he wrote his own.

Another honest mistake is found in John's version of the second burial story, in which he has Joseph and Nicodemus bury Jesus when the female disciples were not present. Therefore, the women would not have known where Jesus was buried. John exposes his error when he has Mary Magdalene go to the tomb on the first day of the week, as if she had seen what Joseph and Nicodemus had done.

A third discrepancy exists in Mark's account. He says that Joseph of Arimathea was a member of the council. Now, according to Mark, all the members of the council agreed that Jesus deserves to die (see Mark 14:64). This means that Joseph of Arimathea condemned Jesus. How could he have been waiting for the Kingdom of God, the central feature of Jesus' message?

It is easy to change a story. What is difficult is to do so without leaving traces of the forgery. When a story is judged unacceptable, it is not so easy to invent another one in its place without betraying oneself. Mark's text illustrates this point with its mention of the day of Preparation. The tradition concerning the first burial survived for some time but was finally lost, while the written texts of the second story survive to this day.

Conclusion

Based on the evidence that I have produced, I conclude that the second burial story, in which Joseph of Arimathea is the central actor, is pious fiction. The body of Jesus must have been disposed of by the Roman soldiers. This is clearly implied, although not explicitly said, in the first story.

The two burial stories illustrate a phenomenon that occurs very frequently in the various narratives concerning what happened during the life of Jesus. Important memories of the past were suppressed. Other events were invented. Traces of those systematic transformations exist in the texts. Some of them are easily recognizable; others are not. This is particularly the case of memories that were repressed and have remained unrecognized to this day.

*

Part One—What happened after the death of Jesus

The Empty Tomb Story

The empty tomb story is based on the second burial story. But if, as I have shown, the second burial story is a pious invention, the empty tomb story must be discarded as a pious invention as well. In other words, the women who are supposed to have discovered the empty tomb and the disciples who are supposed to have been to the empty tomb (Mark 16:1–8; Luke 24:1–12 and John 20:1–18) are the products of pious imagination. We are here in the presence of some form of forged evidence.

But the role of Mary Magdalene does not have to be discarded altogether. Mary could not have gone to the tomb on the first day of the week. The tomb provided by Joseph of Arimathea never existed. The women who witnessed the crucifixion with Mary Magdalene had to leave at sunset on account of the Sabbath. They did not see what the soldiers had done after their departure. Therefore, I cannot exclude the following possibility. On the first day of the week, Mary went to the crucifixion place to see what happened. No traces of the crucifixion were there. What happened to the body of her beloved Jesus? She had to find out. So, she walked around seeking information. But nobody knew what happened to the body of Jesus. She was about to go out of her mind when she felt a presence. This is how her resurrection experience could have started. I will discuss John's text about her resurrection experience in the next section.

*

In our sacred scriptures, the Christian community says itself under the guise of telling the story of Jesus. If it takes great liberties with the historical facts, it is because what matters are not the facts but the Christian faith as it was understood by various communities and evangelists. In other words, there are as many acts of faith as there are believers. This is why it does not matter whether the empty tomb story is a pious fiction or a real fact. The believers do not believe in verifiable facts[6], but in the unfathomable powers of the divine. No matter how we go about them, those powers are beyond our control and even beyond our understanding.

Whatever we say about the resurrection of Jesus is going to be very personal and controversial. Popular representations are unavoidable but can be easily criticized. Any attempt at voiding the mystery is bound to fail.

This does not mean that any attempt at reconstructing what happened during the life of Jesus is useless. This can show how the facts were transformed under the influence of the Easter faith. Most of the time this was done not by choice but by necessity or as faith requires it. Thus, the empty tomb story is not unique. Many important events were manipulated and transformed because they would have made the Christian faith impossible. Others were invented in which the faith recognized itself. This is how our sacred scriptures were produced.

> Being born again in the twenty-first century,
> and seeing the resurrected Christ in the first century
> are religious experiences of the same kind.
> What differs is the historical and religious context.

*

---

6. Verifiable facts fall under the category of knowledge.

Part One—What happened after the death of Jesus

A digression into the Gospel of Matthew

In the Gospel of John, there are two delegations to Pilate, one by the Jewish leadership and one by Joseph of Arimathea. In the Gospel of Matthew there is a third one. This time the high priests and the Pharisees ask Pilate for a favor.

> They said, [63]"Sir, we remember that, during his lifetime, that impostor said, 'I will rise after three days.' [64]So order the tomb to be made secure until the third day. Otherwise his disciples may come and steal him, and then say to the people 'He has risen from the dead,' when the latest imposture will be worse than the first." [65]Pilate said to them, "You have a guard of soldiers; go, make it as secure as you can." [66]So they went with the guard and made the tomb secure by sealing the stone
> Matt 27:63–66

This story has all the features of forgery. It takes for granted that Jesus had indeed predicted his death and resurrection during his life as this is stated in Matthew 16:21–23; 17:22–23 and 20:17–19. But John says that this was not the case. The disciples knew nothing of the fact that, according to the scriptures, he had to rise from among the dead. Here is how John puts it.

When the women told Peter about the empty tomb he went there with John. When John saw the empty tomb, he believed. And the text says,

> "For as yet they did not understand the scripture, that he must rise from the dead."
> John 20:9

The same idea is found in the Gospel of Luke. In his account of what happened with the two disciples who were going back home to Emmaus, Luke says that Jesus initiated them into the Christian mystery by explaining to them that, according to the scriptures, the Messiah was to rise again. "Oh, how foolish you are, and how slow of heart to believe all that the prophets have declared! Was it not necessary that the Messiah should suffer these things and then enter into his glory?" (Luke 24:25–26).

All this shows that the Jewish leadership could not have known about any prediction made by Jesus concerning his resurrection. As we shall see, no such predictions were ever made.

*

Chapter 2

A Spiritual Understanding of the Resurrection in the Gospel of John

In the Gospel of John, the Resurrection of Jesus is discussed in two different sections that are likely to have two different authors. In Chapter 20, the resurrection is discussed under two headings, first, discovery of the empty tomb and apparition to Mary Magdala (20:1–18); second, apparitions to the disciples (20:19–29). In Chapter 14, during the long and intimate exchanges between Jesus and his disciples, there is an allusion to the resurrection experience. This is when the author of those exchanges discusses the reason why Jesus appeared only to his disciples and not to the public (14:22–23). In the first context, the resurrection is described as a physical event. In the second context, it is spoken of as a spiritual event that does not affect the dead body of Jesus.

*

Second text

[22]"What has happened, Master," said Judas (not Judas Iscariot), "that you are going to reveal yourself to us, and not to the world?" [23]"Whoever loves me," Jesus answered,

"will lay my message to heart; and my Father will love him, and we will come to him and make our home with him.
John 14:22–23

After his death, Jesus appeared to his disciples, not to the public. The question that is raised here is, "Why the general public could not see the risen Jesus?"

In its literary context, this question is raised when Jesus was still alive. But if nobody knew during the life of Jesus that, according to scripture, "he must rise from the dead" (John 20:9), the question that is raised here becomes anachronistic. This suggests that all those questions and answers must have taken place in a different context, in which the author of this section of the gospel reproduces exchanges he had with his disciples in a kind of postgraduate seminar. Those theological exchanges must have taken place many years after the death of Jesus. They express the author's theological understanding of the Christian mystery.

Here is how the resurrection experience of the disciples is understood

Those who love Jesus and miss him dearly after his death fulfill the prerequisite condition for seeing him. The Father will love them. He will come with Jesus and dwell in them. Those who are "outside" (see Mark 4:11) are excluded from this intimacy. This excludes not only the public that did not know Jesus, but also those who admired him but stopped following him (see John 6:14–15 and 66).

In other words, this passage recognizes the fact that only a few disciples of Jesus had the privilege of seeing the resurrected Christ. Only they had what it takes to become witnesses to the resurrection. They were predisposed to seeing Jesus. The others were not. Thus, the spiritual and subjective dimension of the resurrection experience is recognized here.

Part One—What happened after the death of Jesus

Trinitarian dimension of the resurrection

> [25] I have told you all this while still with you, [26] but the helper—the Holy Spirit whom the Father will send in my name—will teach you all things, and will recall to your minds all that I have said to you.
> John 14:25–26

The physical presence of Jesus ends with his death. It will be replaced with a spiritual presence, and this spiritual presence will be represented by the Holy Spirit. In other words, Jesus will remain with the disciples under the new form of the Spirit. To see Jesus after his death is to receive the Holy Spirit. What will change is the form in which Jesus is present. Jesus in the flesh will become the vivifying Spirit.

The same thing is said in the following passage.

> [15] If you love me, you will lay my commands to heart, [16] and I will ask the Father, and he will give you another helper, to be with you always—the Spirit of truth. [17] The world cannot receive this Spirit, because it does not see him or recognize him, but you recognize him, because he is always with you, and is within you."
> John 14:15–17

In the same way as the world cannot receive the Spirit, so also it cannot see Jesus after his death.

According to this understanding of what happened after the death of Jesus, there is no need for an empty tomb. The original burial story can be retained. This is so because we are speaking of a spiritual experience that does not involve any physical transformation that affects Jesus' dead body. After his death, Jesus' physical presence was changed into a spiritual presence.

*

A Spiritual Understanding of the Resurrection in the Gospel of John

Is there a contradiction between those two resurrection experiences?

The answer to this question depends on who you ask. For some, the resurrection was a physical event that affected the dead body of Jesus. The empty tomb shows that his body was no longer there. The Jesus who appears to the disciples is not a ghost. His presence is physical. This is how most Christians understand the resurrection. The author of John 14 disagrees. For him the resurrection was a spiritual event that did not affect the dead body of Jesus. Is there a way of going beyond this basic disagreement?

In order to answer this difficult question, I propose to reconstruct the mental processes that could have affected the few disciples who had the privilege of seeing the resurrected Christ. John 14 reconstructs the theological implications of the resurrection. I am interested in reconstructing the mental processes that guided the disciples. In other words, instead of seeking a theological answer, I propose to seek a psychological one.

First, I must recognize that as far as the disciples were concerned, a formidable event occurred that was going to change the course of their lives. They went through a very real transformation. That transformation took place in their minds. They became convinced that Jesus was alive and well. They saw him; they spoke with him; they touched him; he ate with them. At the same time, however, he appeared and disappeared. He could go through closed doors. He was at the same time present and absent. In other words, he did not return to life as things were before his death. If he did, anybody could have seen him.

Now the question that I will raise here is this. Do we know of any situation in which things of that sort can occur? My answer is "Yes." There are people who experience extraordinary things, and those people are known as mystics. Prophets and seers fall in that general category. In the ancient world, communication between heaven and earth took place in the form of dreams and visions.

Part One—What happened after the death of Jesus

> "I will pour out my Spirit upon all flesh, and your sons and your daughters shall prophesy, and your young men shall see visions, and your old men shall dream dreams."
> Acts 2:17

I have quoted here a passage from Acts that is taken from Prophet Joel 2:28. My intention is to show how the prophetic experience was understood in Israel. God sends his Spirit, and those who receive the Spirit become prophets. This is what it takes to make a prophet. But if you want to understand the mode in which the connection is made between God and the people, you must read the second part of the revelation: "Your young men shall see visions, and your old men shall dream dreams." This means that the Spirit acts through visions and dreams.

This is how the phenomenon is described by a prophet who expresses the religious understanding of the phenomenon. But if we want to say the phenomenology of the spiritual experience, we have to reverse the order of things. In this case, what come first are the visions and the dreams. What comes second is the interpretation of those visions and dreams: they are the way God communicates with us humans.

In psychological terms, visions and dreams are produced by our subconscious. The ancients interpreted them as coming from the other world. Today we see their otherness as based on the otherness of the subconscious.

We have here, I think, a good description of the mystical phenomenon. The mystical experience takes many forms. The most common ones involve visions and dreams. At the beginning, the mystics don't know what is happening to them. But after a while, they become sure of themselves. What is happening to them is real and involves some divine intervention. Now the visions they see can be vivid and quite realistic. When this experience is interpreted as caused by God or the Spirit, it becomes a revelation as well as an empowering force.

The case of Paul

In 1 Corinthians 15, 3-11 Paul lists all the apparitions of Jesus then he adds a last one. He says that Jesus appeared to him as he had appeared to the original disciples and empowered him to be an Apostle like them. Now this was a few years after the death of Jesus. Timing is not of the essence for Paul. I would say that many mystics had similar experiences throughout history. They had dreams and visions that had a powerful influence on them. What matters here is the way people interpret their experience. What they see in their visions can be very realistic. Thus, for the disciples of Jesus there is no doubt Christ has appeared to them in a physical mode. This is how they perceived and interpreted what happened. The fact remains, however, that their mystical experience can be a highly subjective one.

Today those who are born again go through a highly transformative experience. I would say that they go through a mini mystical experience.

To go back to the disciples, their vivid recollection of Jesus' apparitions could have been produced by a mystical experience. If this is how we interpret what happened to them, the spiritual nature of their experience becomes clear, and there would be no difference between the realist and the spiritual understanding of the resurrection that are found in the Gospel of John. What appears to us to be different can be compared to the two sides of the same coin. They appear to be different, but they are one and the same; they represent different expressions of the same thing.

*

In the Gospel of John, there are two sets of apparitions to the disciples. The story of Thomas who refused to believe on account of what the other disciples had told him and insisted on seeing Jesus for himself—that story is very interesting. It shows that the mystical experience is collective as well as individual. Sometimes the

Part One—What happened after the death of Jesus

faith of the group is enough to convince its members, but sometimes it is not.

We know from the written testimony of many mystics that, in the beginning, they don't know what is happening to them. But as the same experience repeats itself, they become increasingly sure. At the end, they reach a point of very high certainty, and nothing can shake their faith in what was revealed to them. Here is what Ignatius of Loyola, the founder of the Jesuit Order, said in his autobiography. He speaks of himself in the third person.

> These things which he saw gave him at the time great strength, and were always a striking confirmation of his faith, so much so that he has often thought to himself that if there were no Scriptures to teach us these matters of faith, he was determined to die for them, merely of what he had seen.[1]

Paul and the other Apostles had similar experiences about the resurrected Christ. They became absolutely sure of themselves. But, according to his study of the mystics, Michel de Certeau did not hesitate to speak of the "mystic fable." For him, the mystical experience is real but eminently subjective. A fable is a literary form that can be compared to a parable. Both use fiction to express spiritual views.

I think that what is revealed to the mystics comes from the depth of their unconscious. In relation to the conscious activity of the brain, what is produced by the unconscious seems to come from another world. Thus, "the other world" of the religious experience must be based on the unconscious activity of the brain that manifests itself through dreams and visions.

In other words, dualism is rooted in the human mind. What is conscious refers to this world and what is unconscious refers to the other world. There is also a collective and social consciousness. Members of the group must conform to the group. Thus, religions and political systems demand and easily obtain the submission of the individual. Islam is not the only religion in which submission

---

1. Quoted by W.W.Meissner, S.J., M.D. in *Ignatius of Loyola, the psychology of a saint*, Yale University Press, 1992, 83.

to God is essential. Religious and political formations are based on the collective unconscious. Some mobility is possible, but it comes at a price that is often prohibitive.

*

The special case of Mary Magdalene

In the Gospel of John, Mary Magdalene represents the ideal disciple. She was deeply in love with Jesus, religiously and emotionally. Therefore, she was deeply affected by the death of her beloved Lord.

When the sun was setting and the sabbath was about to begin, she had to leave the crucifixion place. Early on the first day of the week, she went back there but all the traces of the crucifixions had been removed. So, she went looking for information. Her main concern was with the body of Jesus. She needed to know where the body was in order to start the mourning process. Perhaps she wanted to give Jesus an honorable burial. But she was unable to get any information. She was going to go out of her mind when she felt a presence. First, she did not know what or who it was. She was saved when she realized that it was the Lord.

This description of what happened is typical of a spiritual experience as John 14 speaks about it.

*

Part One—What happened after the death of Jesus

Christian dualism

This dualism is partially recognized by Gospel scholars who distinguish between the historical Jesus and the Christ of the faith. The Christ of the faith is produced by the apostolic faith in the resurrection, which transforms Jesus into a celestial being. But the historical Jesus was just a man. When he died, his death was final. The faith in his resurrection is an act of his disciples. They sincerely believed that God had resurrected him. But their resurrection experience was purely spiritual and subjective. It did not affect the dead body of Jesus.

Freud said that Judaism is a religion of the Father and Christianity a religion of the Son. There is some truth here, but only a partial truth. The religion of Jesus was a religion of the Father. He was 100% Jewish. His prayer, the *Our Father*, does not mention the Son at all. After his death, the disciples invented the Christian religion and made it a religion of the Son. As it exists today, Christianity combines the religion of the Father with the religion of the Son.

I claim that this development was made over the dead body of Jesus. During his life, he had forcefully refused to take the lead of a Messianic movement. This caused him to lose his popularity in Galilee.

I will discuss this point in the Second Part of this book.

*

Chapter 3

Apparitions' Stories

I will discuss here the apparition's stories in the Gospel of John. I will discuss Luke's apparition to the disciples of Emmaus in the Second Part in connection with the notion of successful initiations into the Christian mystery.

*

Mary Magdalene

The apparitions' stories begin with Mary Magdalene. After the mandatory Sabbath rest, she left very early and went to the tomb to mourn her beloved Jesus.

> ¹On the first day of the week, early in the morning, while it was still dark, Mary of Magdala went to the tomb, and saw that the stone had been removed. ²So she came running to Simon Peter, and to that other disciple who was Jesus' friend, and said to them, "They have taken away the Master out of the tomb, and we do not know where they have laid him!"
> John 20:1–2

Part One—What happened after the death of Jesus

Peter and the other disciple ran to the tomb and saw that it was empty. Then they returned home. In the meantime, Mary came back. She had to find the body of Jesus.

> [11] Meanwhile Mary was standing close outside the tomb, weeping. Still weeping, she leant forward into the tomb, [12] and perceived two angels clothed in white sitting there, where the body of Jesus had been lying, one where the head and the other where the feet had been. [13] "Why are you weeping?" asked the angels. "They have taken my Master away," she answered, "and I do not know where they have laid him." [14] After saying this, she turned around, and looked at Jesus standing there, but she did not know that it was Jesus. [15] "Why are you weeping? Whom are you seeking?" he asked. Supposing him to be the gardener, Mary answered, "If it was you, Sir, who carried him away, tell me where you have laid him, and I will take him away myself."
>
> [16] "Mary!" said Jesus. She turned around, and exclaimed in Hebrew, "Rabboni!" (or, as we should say, 'teacher'). [17] "Do not hold me," Jesus said, "for I have not yet ascended to the Father. But go to my brothers, and tell them that I am ascending to him who is my Father and their Father, my God and their God." [18] Mary of Magdala went and told the disciples that she had seen the Master, and that he had said this to her.
>
> John 20:11–18

Mary was deeply in love with Jesus. His death was the worst catastrophe that could happen to her. She worshipped him. Had it not been for her, the resurrection of Christ would have not materialized in the minds of the disciples, and his story would have ended with his death.

Some may say that if she had not been first at the empty tomb, someone else would have and the Christian faith would have started.

This objection can be made if one assumes that Jesus was really buried by Joseph of Arimathea. But if we believe that Jesus was buried by the Roman soldiers in an unmarked grave that remained unknown to the public, the burial by Joseph of Arimathea becomes a pious fiction. This is why I would reconstruct what happened in the following way.

On Sunday morning, Mary went to the crucifixion place in order to find out what happened to the body of Jesus. But no traces of the crucifixions were left. So, she went looking for information. But nobody could help her. She was going to go out of her mind, when suddenly she felt a presence. This is how her mystical experience started. She was so vulnerable that her mystical experience saved her from total madness. Her distress was transformed into joyous relief. The situation was totally reversed, and Mary became the first Apostle (envoy with a special message). She felt empowered to inform the male disciples and was able to induce their personal mystical experiences.

This reconstruction is based on what we know about the mystical experience as it is discussed by Michel de Certeau in *The Mystic Fable*, translated from French by Michael B. Smith, the University of Chicago Press, 1992.

The mystical experience can be communicated. There are schools of mystics as there are schools of prophets. Sometimes communication fails as in the case of Judas.

The best example of the transmission of the faith is the fact that religions survive by transmission of the faith from generation to generation. Every act of faith in any religion is based on a mini mystical experience. A good way to illustrate this phenomenon can be found in John's story of the Samaritan woman. She introduced Jesus to her folks as a possible Messiah. First, they believed on account of her testimony, but after a few days they told her, "It is no longer because of what you said that we believe, for we have heard for ourselves, and we know that this is truly the Savior of the world." (John 4:42)

Because mystical and spiritual experiences can be transmitted to others exactly as faith can be transmitted, what counts is the testimony of a trustworthy person. Thus, Mary Magdalene's encounter with the resurrected Christ started the transmission process of the faith in the resurrection, first to the disciples and then beyond them to the believers.

Part One—What happened after the death of Jesus

This reconstruction of what is likely to have happened to Mary Magdalene is typical of a spiritual experience as John 14 speaks of it.

Here is what Michel de Certeau said about this incident. He was following the second burial story by Joseph of Arimathea.

> Before the empty tomb stood Mary Magdalene, that eponymous figure of the modern mystic. "I do not know where they have put him." She questions a passerby: "If you are the one who carried him off, tell me where you have laid him."[1] That question, articulated by the entire primitive community, was not limited to one circumstance. It structured the apostolic discourse. In the Gospel of John, Jesus has no presence other than that which is divided between historical places in which he no longer is, and the unknowable place, says Jesus, "Where I am."[2] His "being there" is the paradox of "having been" here previously, of remaining inaccessibly elsewhere and of "coming back" later. His body is structured by dissemination, like a text. Since that time, the believers have continued to wonder: "Where art thou?" And from century to century they ask history as it passes: "Where have you put him" With events that are murmurings come from afar, with Christian discourses that codify the hermeneutics of new experiences, with community practices that render present a *"caritas"*, they invent a mystic body—missing and sought after—that would also be their own[3].

Thus, the Christian discourse about Jesus is, of necessity, paradoxical.

*

1. John 20:13 and 15.
2. See John 7:34 and 36; 12:26; 14:3, 17, 24; etc.
3. Michel de Certeau, *The Mystic Fable*, translated by Michael B. Smith, the University of Chicago Press, 1992. 81–82.

Apparitions to the disciples

The disciples' faith in the resurrection was based not only on what Mary had told them but it was also confirmed by the visions that they had of the resurrected Christ.

First apparition

> [19] In the evening of the same day—the first day of the week—after the doors of the room, in which the disciples were, had been shut because they were afraid of the religious authorities, Jesus came and stood among them and said, "Peace be with you"; [20] after which he showed them his hands and his side. The disciples were filled with joy when they saw the Master. [21] Again Jesus said to them, "Peace be with you. As the Father has sent me as his messenger, so I am sending you." [22] After saying this, he breathed on them, and said, "Receive the Holy Spirit; [23] if you remit anyone's sins, they have been remitted; and, if you retain them, they have been retained."
> John 20:19-23

First, let me say that there is a big difference between the resurrection of Lazarus and the resurrection of Jesus (see John 11:1-44). Lazarus was revived and returned to physical life. Everybody could have seen him and recognized him. The revived Lazarus had not become immortal. Eventually he would have died. Jesus, on the other hand, did not return to physical life. His death was final. This made it possible for him to enter the divine realm and ascend to the Father.

The apparition is described in concrete and physical terms. Jesus speaks and the disciples can hear him. He showed them the crucifixion marks on his hands and his side. At the same time, however, his body is not real. He can go through closed doors. He appears and disappears. This combination of real and unreal features is characteristic of dreams.

Part One—What happened after the death of Jesus

A similar thing can be said about Mary Magdalene's experience. First, she does not recognize Jesus. She thinks he is the gardener. But when Jesus says her name, she recognizes him. We shall see that a similar thing happened to the two Emmaus disciples. First, they don't recognize Jesus. But when he broke the bread, they recognized him, and he disappeared. All this suggests that the apparitions are produced, like dreams, by our subconscious. In comparison with the conscious world, the subconscious is the other world.

The second feature of this apparition is the empowerment of the disciples. Jesus breathes on them and gives them the Spirit. The Spirit gives the disciples the intelligence they need to understand the Christian mystery. Jesus' physical presence ends with his death. After that, his presence became spiritual. In this way, the Christian mystery was internalized. The conscious and the subconscious worlds became unified and inseparable.

Second apparition

[26] A week later, his disciples were again in the house, and Thomas was with them. Although the doors were shut, Jesus came and stood among them and said, "Peace be with you." [27] Then he said to Thomas, "Put your finger here and see my hands. Reach out your hand and put it in my side. Do not doubt but believe." [28] Thomas answered him, "My Lord and my God!" [29] Jesus said to him, "Have you believed because you have seen me? Blessed are those who have not seen and yet have come to believe."

[26] A week later the disciples were again in the house, and Thomas was with them. After the doors had been shut, Jesus came and stood among them, and said, "Peace be with you." [27] Then he said to Thomas, "Place your finger here, and look at my hands; and place your hand here, and put it into my side; and do not refuse to believe, but believe." [28] And Thomas exclaimed, "My Master, and my God!" [29] "Is it because you have seen me that you have

believed?" said Jesus. "Blessed are they who have not seen, and yet have believed!"
John 20:24–29

This story shows that the recognition of the resurrection was not instantaneous but progressive. It must have taken time to convince all the members of the group. As I said before, the spiritual experience can be communicated and shared, especially when we are talking about people who are very close and share the same dream. This was the case with the disciples. But even then, it seems that Judas betrayed the group because he could not believe in the resurrection. The story of his collaboration with the Jewish authorities is a vicious fabrication.

*

Appendix—Apparition at the lakeshore

The Gospel of John has two endings. The second ending (chapter 21) is a late addition to the text. It tells about a last apparition of Jesus at the lakeshore. The first author of that gospel had recently died, which caused a problem to that community. The rumor had circulated that he would not die before the return of Christ and the end of the world. The author of the second ending wanted to show that this rumor was incorrect.

The return of the resurrected Christ was expected to be imminent in the early years of the Christian movement. But as this return failed to materialize, the faith of the believers was shaken. This was a weak point in the original expectation. It should have shown that the Christian faith in the resurrected Christ was mistaken. But, once the faith had become firmly held, nothing could have disproved it. Difficulties of this nature are easily overcome by believers. Today, it has become evident that the return of Christ is a pious myth. It is always risky to predict the future.

I will call the author of chapter 21 John 2 to distinguish him from the author of the main gospel, John 1.

Part One—What happened after the death of Jesus

There is another timing problem with the story of John 2. It takes place after John 1 had died, which is usually dated around the year 100 AD. That's more than sixty years after the death of Jesus. Peter was dead, and so were most of the original disciples.

Most likely John 2 is telling here a story that took place weeks after the death of Jesus. Peter and a few other disciples went fishing. They were fishermen by trade.

> [1]Later on, Jesus showed himself again to the disciples by the Sea of Tiberias. [2]It was in this way,—Simon Peter, Thomas, who was called 'The Twin,' Nathanael of Cana in Galilee, Zebedee's sons, and two other disciples of Jesus, were together, when Simon Peter said, [3]"I am going fishing." "We will come with you," said the others. They went out and got into the boat, but caught nothing that night. [4]Just as day was breaking, Jesus came and stood on the beach; but the disciples did not know that it was he. [5]"My children," he said, "have you anything to eat?" "No," they answered. [6]"Cast your net to the right of the boat," he said, "and you will find fish." So they cast the net, and now they could not haul it in because of the quantity of fish. [7]The disciple whom Jesus loved said to Peter, "It is the Master!" When Simon Peter heard that it was the Master, he fastened his coat around him (for he had taken it off) and threw himself into the sea. [8]But the rest of the disciples came in the boat (for they were only about a hundred yards from shore), dragging the net full of fish. [9]When they had come ashore, they found a charcoal fire ready, with some fish already on it, and some bread as well. [10]"Bring some of the fish which you have just caught," said Jesus. [11]So Simon Peter got into the boat and hauled the net ashore full of large fish, a hundred and fifty-three of them; and yet, although there were so many, the net had not been torn. [12]"Come and have breakfast", Jesus said. None of the disciples dared ask him who he was, because they knew it was the Master. [13]Jesus went and took the bread and gave it to them, and the fish too. [14]This was the third time that Jesus showed himself to the disciples after he had risen from the dead.

Apparitions' Stories

¹⁵When breakfast was over, Jesus said to Simon Peter, "Simon, son of John, do you love me more than the others?" "Yes, Master," he answered, "you know that I am your friend." "Feed my lambs," said Jesus. ¹⁶Then, a second time, Jesus asked, "Simon, son of John, do you love me?" "Yes, Master," he answered, "you know that I am your friend." "Tend my sheep," said Jesus. ¹⁷The third time, Jesus said to him, "Simon, son of John, are you my friend?" Peter was hurt at his third question being 'Are you my friend?'; and exclaimed, "Master, you know everything! You can tell that I am your friend." "Feed my sheep," said Jesus. ¹⁸"In truth I tell you," he continued, "when you were young, you used to put on your own clothes, and walk wherever you wished; but, when you have grown old, you will have to stretch out your hands, while someone else puts on your clothes, and takes you where you do not wish." ¹⁹Jesus said this to show the death by which Peter was to honor God, and then he added, "Follow me"
John 21:1–19

The disciples don't recognize Jesus

This is a recurring feature in many apparition stories. Mary Magdalene recognized Jesus when he said her name. The two Emmaus disciples recognized Jesus when he broke the bread (see Luke 24:30–31). In this last apparition story, Jesus is recognized by the perceptive disciple, the one that Jesus loved.

Peter is now Jesus' successor

"Tend my sheep."

The empowerment of the disciples is another feature of the apparitions. Here is what we read in Matthew.

¹⁶The eleven disciples went to Galilee, to the mountain where Jesus told them to meet him; ¹⁷and, when they saw him, they bowed to the ground before him; although

Part One—What happened after the death of Jesus

some felt doubtful. [18]Then Jesus came up, and spoke to them, saying, "All authority in heaven and on the earth has been given to me. [19]Therefore go and make disciples of all the nations, baptizing them in the name of the Father, the Son, and the Holy Spirit, [20]and teaching them to lay to heart all the commands that I have given you; and, remember, I myself am with you every day until the close of the age."

Matt 28:16–20

The doubting feature is not unique to Thomas. According to Matthew, when the disciples saw the resurrected Jesus, some of them doubted (see verse 17). The resurrection experience was doubtful, in the beginning. As it was repeated, the disciples became sure of themselves. This feature is characteristic of the mystical experience as it is discussed in the *Mystic Fable*.

*

PART TWO

What happened during the life of Jesus.

1—Memories that are repressed in the Gospel of Mark
2—Stories that were transformed or invented after the death of Jesus.

*

Part Two—What happened during the life of Jesus.

The trial of Jesus in the Koran

After his death, Jesus appeared before the divine tribunal. God asked him, "Did you say to the people 'Consider me and my mother as gods of lesser rank than God?' " Jesus answered, "Be you glorified, I could not have uttered what was not right... I told them only what you commanded me to say, that you shall worship God, my Lord and your Lord" (See Koran 5:116–118).

Ideas of this kind existed in the early days of the Christian movement among those who recognized Jesus as a prophet but would not deify him. They claimed that Jesus was deified after his death by those disciples who believed in his resurrection. His mother was eventually proclaimed "Mother of God" by the Council of Ephesus (AD 431).

As we shall see in this second part, the Gospel of Mark confirms that Jesus did not proclaim himself Messiah and Son of God and that he even violently rejected the idea. But Mark's narrative does so covertly and in ways that confuse us instead of enlightening us. In other words, there are in the Gospel of Mark secret revelations that have not been recognized to this day. This makes my book, at the same time, very controversial, utterly unorthodox and highly innovative. In reality, I just repeat old ideas but add to them the preposterous claim that they are confirmed by the Gospel of Mark. All that is needed is to know how to read a text—something that gospel scholarship has not mastered yet. I am not speaking here of ordinary texts, but of "texts that hide what they know."

*

Chapter 1

Repressed Memories in the Gospel of Mark

A story

A young boy saw his dad kill his mother. But life continued as if no murder was committed. The boy had no choice but to live with his father. So, he repressed the memory of the murder. When he became a young adult, he started having psychological problems. He was cured when the analyst helped him remember what had happened.

Another story

I live now in a retirement home. Sometimes we meet in the lounge and chat over a cup of coffee. A few weeks ago, a friend asked me what I was working on. I told him about my interest in repressed memories and how they return unexpectedly. He reacted very vividly. He told me that he knew about repressed memories. When he was a child, he said, he lived with his dad and stepmother. Both were abusive. His stepmother used to beat him up when he came back from school and lock him up in a dark closet until his dad

Part Two—What happened during the life of Jesus.

came back from work. Recently, that is more than sixty years after the facts, he felt the need to revisit that house. He Googled the address and found out that the house was on the market. So, he took a virtual tour. When he arrived at the closet, he remembered what his stepmother used to do to him. For some reason, he had forgotten all those incidents. He recovered his old memories at a time when he could cope with the fact that he was abused.

Freud and repressed memories

Freud discovered that repressed memories return in subtle ways, and that when this phenomenon is recognized, it can reveal what was repressed in the first place. People repress certain memories, when those memories are (or become later) threatening and intolerable. They do it unconsciously. In the absence of any therapy, they die with their secret. But if they were to recall the past orally or in writing, and if we have a reliable account of their oral reminiscences, we should look for clues in their narrative that can take us back to what was repressed. When repressed memories return, they do so under a disguise. It takes some skills to recognize what is going on.

I propose to apply this technique to two enigmatic texts in the Gospel of Mark.

*

Two enigmatic texts in the Gospel of Mark

In the Gospel of Mark, we are told that Jesus fed five and four thousand people in a miraculous way. The first enigmatic text occurs right after the first miraculous feeding and refers directly to it (Mark 6:52). The second enigmatic text occurs right after the second miraculous feeding and refers to those two miracles (Mark 8:17–21). Thus, a direct connection exists between the two enigmatic texts and those two miracles.

First Miracle of the Loaves

³⁰When the apostles came back to Jesus, they told him all that they had done and all that they had taught. ³¹"Come by yourselves privately to some lonely spot," he said, "and rest for a while"—for there were so many people coming and going that they had not time even to eat. ³²So they set off privately in their boat for a lonely spot. ³³Many people saw them going, and recognized them, and from all the towns they flocked together to the place on foot, and got there before them. ³⁴On getting out of the boat, Jesus saw a great crowd, and his heart was moved at the sight of them, because they were like sheep without a shepherd; and he began to teach them many things. ³⁵When it grew late, his disciples came up to him, and said, "This is a lonely spot, and it is already late. ³⁶Send the people away, so that they may go to the farms and villages around and buy themselves something to eat." ³⁷But Jesus answered, "It is for you to give them something to eat." "Are we to go and spend almost a year's wages on bread," they asked, "to give them to eat?" ³⁸"How many loaves have you?" he asked, "Go, and see." When they had found out, they told him, "Five, and two fish." ³⁹Jesus directed them to make all the people take their seats on the green grass, in parties; ⁴⁰and they sat down in groups—in hundreds, and in fifties. ⁴¹Taking the five loaves and the two fish, Jesus looked up to heaven, and said the blessing; he broke the loaves into pieces, and gave them to his disciples for them to serve out to the people, and he divided the two fish also among them all. ⁴²Everyone had sufficient to eat; ⁴³and they picked up enough broken pieces to fill twelve baskets, as well as some of the fish. ⁴⁴The people who ate the bread were five thousand in number.

Mark 6:30–44

Jesus walks on the sea

⁴⁵Immediately afterward Jesus made his disciples get into the boat, and cross over in advance, in the direction of

Part Two—What happened during the life of Jesus.

Bethsaida, while he himself was dismissing the crowd. ⁴⁶After he had taken leave of the people, he went away up the hill to pray. ⁴⁷When evening fell, the boat was out in the middle of the sea, and Jesus on the shore alone. ⁴⁸Seeing them laboring at the oars—for the wind was against them—about three hours after midnight Jesus came towards them, walking on the water, intending to join them. ⁴⁹But, when they saw him walking on the water, they thought it was a ghost, and cried out; ⁵⁰for all of them saw him, and were terrified. But Jesus at once spoke to them. "Courage!" he said, "it is I; do not be afraid!" ⁵¹Then he got into the boat with them, and the wind dropped. The disciples were utterly amazed, ⁵²for they had not understood about the loaves, but their hearts were hardened.

Mark 6:30–52

We have here two stories that follow one another and are connected by verse 52, the miraculous feeding of the five thousand and Jesus walking on the sea.

The enigmatic text is in verse 52

What is strange about this verse is that it is set in the context of Jesus walking on the sea, which is totally different from the context of the miraculous feeding of the five thousand people. One context is pre-Pascal and the other context is post-Pascal. Is pre-Pascal what happened during the earthly life of Jesus. Is post-Pascal what happened after his death. The apparition of Jesus walking on the sea has all the features of a post-pascal apparition that is set in a pre-Pascal context. The Gospel of Mark plays on those two registers all the time. We shall see, in our future explorations, that it keeps confusing those two very different contexts.

The incident of the apparition of Jesus walking on the water has some features that are typical of many apparition stories. First Jesus is not recognized. Second, he has extraordinary powers. When he got into the boat, the storm ended. Jesus appears to be a ghost, but he is real. This dual feature is also typical of many apparitions.

The interpretation of verse 52 is going to depend on whether it says something that materialized after the death of Jesus or during his life. Its post-Easter context suggests that it deals with a problem that materialized after the death of Jesus. Now it is clear that Mark's narrative wants us to believe that the nightly apparition of Jesus took place during his life and on the very night that followed the first miraculous feeding. At the same time, however, the narrative gives us some clues that suggest the contrary. This makes verse 52 problematic.

Verse 52 says two things about the disciples. Their hearts were hardened, and they could not understand something important about the loaves.

The hardening of the heart is reminiscent of what God did to Pharaoh in the book of Exodus. God hardened the heart of the Egyptian king so that he would not collaborate with Moses and let the Hebrew people go. We are to assume that a similar occult force affected the disciples and prevented them from understanding what was there to understand. So far, so good. But we still cannot identify what the disciples could not understand about the miracle of the loaves. This is what makes verse 52 so enigmatic.

What if a mysterious force made them alter an important feature of that meal?

Let us see if the second enigmatic text can shed some light on this question.

*

Second enigmatic text

The second text occurs right after the second miraculous feeding. It refers to the two miraculous feedings and implies that the disciples had serious problems with them. But those problems are not identified. This makes the text enigmatic.

Part Two—What happened during the life of Jesus.

Second Miraculous Feeding

About that time, when there was again a great crowd of people who had nothing to eat, Jesus called his disciples to him, and said, ²"My heart is moved at the sight of all these people, for they have already been with me three days and they have nothing to eat; ³and if I send them away to their homes hungry, they will break down on the way; and some of them have come a long distance." ⁴"Where will it be possible," his disciples answered, "to get sufficient bread for these people in this lonely place?" ⁵"How many loaves have you?" he asked. "Seven," they answered. ⁶Jesus told the crowd to sit down on the ground. Then he took the seven loaves, and, after saying the thanksgiving, broke them, and gave them to his disciples to serve out; and they served them out to the crowd. ⁷They had also a few small fish; and, after he had said the blessing, he told the disciples to serve out these as well. ⁸The people had sufficient to eat, and they picked up seven baskets full of the broken pieces that were left. ⁹There were about four thousand people. Then Jesus dismissed them. ¹⁰Immediately afterward, getting into the boat with his disciples, Jesus went to the district of Dalmanutha.

Mark 8:1–10

The disciples' problem

¹¹Here the Pharisees came out, and began to argue with Jesus, asking him for some sign from the heavens, to test him. ¹²Sighing deeply, Jesus said, "Why does this generation ask for a sign? I tell you, no sign will be given it." ¹³So he left them to themselves, and, getting into the boat again, went away to the opposite shore.

¹⁴Now the disciples had forgotten to take any bread with them, one loaf being all that they had in the boat. ¹⁵So Jesus gave them this warning. "Take care," he said, "beware of the leaven of the Pharisees and the leaven of Herod." ¹⁶They began talking to one another about their

being short of bread; ¹⁷and, noticing this, Jesus said to them, "Why are you talking about your being short of bread? Don't you yet see or understand? Are your hearts hardened? ¹⁸Though you have eyes, do you not see? And though you have ears, do you not hear? Don't you remember, ¹⁹when I broke up the five loaves for the five thousand, how many baskets of broken pieces you picked up?" "Twelve," they said. ²⁰"And when the seven for the four thousand, how many basketfuls of broken pieces did you pick up?" "Seven," they said. ²¹"Don't you understand now?" he repeated.

Mark 8:11–21

This second enigmatic text (verses 17 to 21) is set in a pre-Easter context. But it has a lot in common with the first enigmatic text. In both cases we are told that the disciples had an understanding problem and that their hearts were hardened. Because of this, I would say that verses 17 to 21 must be classified as post-Easter. This means that the disciples' problem with the two miraculous feedings materialized after the death of Jesus.

When we read those enigmatic texts as if they say what happened during the life of Jesus and right after the two miraculous meals, they make no sense at all. Luke and Matthew recognized this point and did something about it.

*

Part Two—What happened during the life of Jesus.

How Matthew and Luke dealt with those enigmatic texts

Both Matthew and Luke used Mark as their principal source of information about what happened during the life of Jesus. We can say that their gospels were revised and augmented versions of Mark.

It goes without saying that our two enigmatic texts did not make any sense to them. Luke discarded the entire story of Jesus walking on the sea with the strange remark of verse 52. He discarded the second miraculous feeding as well as the enigmatic text that followed it. Matthew discarded the first enigmatic text (verse 52). He kept the incident in which Jesus warns the disciples about the Pharisees. But he transformed the story in such a way so he could explain what Jesus had in mind. Here is his text.

> ⁵Now the disciples had crossed to the opposite shore, and had forgotten to take any bread. ⁶Presently Jesus said to them, "Take care and be on your guard against the leaven of the Pharisees and Sadducees." ⁷But the disciples began talking among themselves about their having brought no bread. ⁸On noticing this, Jesus said, "Why are you talking among yourselves about your being short of bread, you of little faith? 9Don't you yet see, nor remember the five loaves for the five thousand, and how many baskets you took away? ¹⁰Nor yet the seven loaves for the four thousand, and how many basketfuls you took away? ¹¹How is it that you do not see that I was not speaking about bread? Be on your guard against the leaven of the Pharisees and Sadducees." ¹²Then they understood that he had told them to be on their guard, not against the leaven of bread, but against the teaching of the Pharisees and Sadducees.
>
> Matt 16:5–12

In his verse 12 Matthew resolved the riddle. Jesus was not talking of bread, but of the teaching of the Pharisees and Sadducees.

In the end, Matthew and Luke eliminated Mark's enigmatic texts. This is a good way of eliminating a problem. Today we do not feel free to correct Mark's text and we don't know what his text means. We tend to play it safe and ignore the problem. Most scholars follow this path.

*

William Wrede

In his famous book published in 1901, *The Messianic Secret*, the German scholar, William Wrede, identified Mark's two enigmatic texts[1]. He recognized in them something important that deserves special attention. But he did not have any clue about the function that they play in the Gospel of Mark.

He took it for granted that Mark had invented those nonsensical stories. But what could have made Mark so different from Matthew and Luke? Did he lack all sense of logic? Were they normal, but Mark abnormal? Another possibility exists. Mark could have received those stories from a respectable source. He reproduced them as he had received them, because he did not feel free to correct his source. According to this second scenario, the source of Mark must have been highly respectable and must have had a disturbed mind.

Unfortunately, many gospel scholars continue to follow Wrede's prejudiced view. Another question is related to this one. According to Papias (early second century), Peter was the source of Mark. But Papias was criticized because his theological views were not "correct. The problem is that what he said about Peter and Mark has nothing to do with theological speculation. In this case, Papias was recalling some information that he had received. No extraordinary intelligence is required to transmit this kind of

---

1. William Wrede, *The Messianic Secret*, translated by J.C.G. Greig, James Clarke & Co, LTD, Cambridge and London, 1971, 103. He writes, "Two passages, however, still require special emphasis: 6.50–52 and 8.16–21." Unfortunately, Wrede attributes to Mark the invention of those two passages without explaining why someone in his right mind would invent such nonsense. Are we to assume that Mark had a totally different logic than Matthew and Luke?

Part Two—What happened during the life of Jesus.

information and one does not have to be theologically correct in order to transmit what he was told.

Here is what Eusebius wrote about what Papias said about Mark.

> "Mark, having become the interpreter of Peter, wrote down accurately, though not indeed in order, whatsoever he remembered of the things done or said by Christ. For he neither heard the Lord nor followed him, but afterward, as I said, he followed Peter, who adapted his teaching to the needs of his hearers, but with no intention of giving a connected account of the Lord's discourses, so that Mark committed no error while he thus wrote some things as he remembered them. For he was careful of one thing, not to omit any of the things which he had heard, and not to state any of them falsely."[2]

The interpretation of the Gospel of Mark differs greatly whether we assume that Peter was his principal source or not. We shall see that only an eyewitness who knew what happened during the life of Jesus could have repressed some crucial memories that would have made his Easter faith untenable. Mark was not an eyewitness; therefore, he could not have repressed memories he never had. Therefore, he must have reproduced the testimony of an eyewitness, namely Peter.

*

2. Eusebius, *Ecclesiastical History*, 3. 39.

Note on repressed memories

Today there is a debate among psychoanalysts about repressed memories and the way analysts can help their patients remember what they had repressed. Many think that in some cases the analysts suggest things to their patients (such as having been abused when a child) and induce them (without meaning it) to imagine facts that did not take place. I suppose that this is possible in some cases. But this is likely to be the exception, not the rule.

I am not a psychoanalyst. I have no clients and I am not in the business of curing people. I speak of memories that were repressed some two thousand years ago and have remained repressed to this day. The technique that I use to identify repressed memories is based on what Freud has discovered, namely that memories that have been repressed return, not overtly but covertly, and in bits and pieces, in the discourse of the person who has repressed them.

I suspect that we have in our two enigmatic texts a return of the repressed memories. This is what makes them so enigmatic. If I am right, the return of the repressed must reveal what was repressed. The most precious information that I can deduce from our texts is that the disciples had a big problem with the two miraculous meals. But the nature of their problem remains unknown.

When memories are repressed, this takes place unconsciously. Similarly, the return of the repressed takes place unconsciously.

William Wrede had no way of knowing what Freud was going to discover about repressed memories. He believed that Mark's Gospel was created by Mark, and that Mark was responsible for the contradictions that are found in it. The historical critical method has no way of identifying Mark's sources from the study of his texts. In this regard, the psychoanalytical approach is much more advanced. It can identify his sources from his texts. Consequently, Wrede rejected the story of Papias. He believed that Mark's narrative does not corroborate what that unreliable writer says. His problem was that he did not know anything about repressed memories and the return of the repressed, a phenomenon that must go back to an eyewitness, because only an eyewitness knows what

Part Two—What happened during the life of Jesus.

happened during the life of Jesus and can have reasons to repress disturbing memories—memories that contradict the Pascal faith and render it unsustainable.

*

Let Mark's texts speak for themselves

Hardening of the Heart

Please allow me to go back to what I have already said about the hardening of the heart. In the Biblical book of Exodus, the same expression is used. God is said to have hardened the heart of Pharaoh. In this case God acts as a mysterious force that controls Pharaoh and makes him resist the divine orders. The hardening of the heart seems to occur when there is a serious conflict. Those who are affected by it behave as if they were under the influence of forces that controlled them and over which they had no control.

In the book of Exodus, we know the problem with which Pharaoh was confronted. In the case of the disciples, we don't know what could have caused the hardening of their hearts. We do not see any conflict that could have affected them and caused them to resist (like Pharaoh). This is why the hardening of their hearts does not make any sense to us.

But what if they had a serious problem that they could not recognize? In other words, what if they had repressed all memories related to that unknown and unrecognized problem? In this case, all we have to do is identify what they had repressed.

Inability to understand

The first text says that the disciples did not understand something about the loaves. But it does not tell us what they could not understand, and we don't see what was there to understand. As we shall see later, instead of enlightening us, this statement confuses us even more. Its purpose is to hide the problem instead of identifying it. One thing is clear, however. There is a connection between the disciples' inability to understand and the first miracle of the loaves. They must have had a problem with the way they reported the first miraculous meal.

Speaking of the disciples' inability to understand, many interpreters propose an explanation of the following kind. They say

Part Two—What happened during the life of Jesus.

in substance that the disciples did not really know at that point in time who Jesus really was. Reference is made here to the divine nature of Jesus as it was going to be revealed after the resurrection. If he could feed five and four thousand people in a miraculous way, the disciples should not have worried about having no bread. This interpretation takes for granted that the two collective meals were miraculous as reported, and that, unlike other miracles or much better than them, they revealed the "divine" nature of Jesus.

We are going to see that the disciples became aware of the "divine" identity of Jesus after their resurrection experience and the pouring of the Spirit that enlightened them. But to assume that what was at stake in those two enigmatic texts is the identity of Jesus is not supported by the texts. The texts clearly link the problem to the collective meals and blame the disciples for not understanding and not remembering something important that was related to those meals.

Memory Problem

The second text speaks not only of their inability to understand but also of their inability to remember.

> 8—[17]"Why are you talking about having no bread?
> Do you still not perceive or understand?
> Are your hearts hardened?
> [18]Do you have eyes, and fail to see? Do you have ears, and fail to hear?"
> And do you not remember?

This problem was not mentioned in the first text. In the second text, Jesus blames them for their inability to remember what had happened very recently. But when he tested their memory, their answers were correct. They knew about the leftovers that they had collected at the end of the two meals (See 8: 19–20). Despite that, Jesus maintained that they had a memory problem (see verse 21).

In the second text, the one who is not making sense is Jesus. He assaults the disciples in highly unfair ways. If they don't understand and don't remember, all he had to do was enlighten them.

It seems to me that the Jesus who assaults the disciples in this story is highly abnormal. Consequently, I would say that we have here a very strange situation. Jesus as well as the disciples had serious problems. At this point I have no clue related to Jesus' problem. But I have three clues that are related to the disciples' problem.

1 — Their hearts are hardened. Consequently, they have eyes and fail to see; they have ears and fail to hear.

2 – They have an understanding problem that is related to the two miraculous feeding.

3 — They have a memory problem that is related to the same meals.

Let me concentrate on the memory problem

If the disciples had a memory problem that was related to the two collective meals, that problem could not have materialized right after the two meals. Normally memory problems occur after the passing of time or after a traumatic event. Now no traumatic event occurred right after the two meals. Therefore, the disciples' problem must have materialized later in time and most likely after the death of Jesus. Their traumatic experience must have occurred after they had become witnesses to the resurrection and the definers of the Christian faith. Something in those two collective meals must have become radically incompatible with the Easter faith. Because of that, their memory of the two meals was altered, not by choice but by necessity. This is why they speak of their problem as hardening of the heart.

On the other hand, the texts confirm my view. They most clearly say that the disciples had serious problems. The texts say so. They don't allow for any other understanding. But this is not all. The two texts make it perfectly clear that the disciples' problem

Part Two—What happened during the life of Jesus.

was directly connected to the two miraculous meals. This suggests that there is something wrong with the way those two stories were reported. The question is, "What could that be?"

Here I have to proceed as detectives do. They make an educated guess and then they see if the guess fits. Now the two meals are described as miracles. What if this was not the case? What if those meals were organized and the people had come with plenty of food for the entire day?

Let's examine this possibility.

*

Jesus organized the first collective meal with the help of his disciples

Here is how Mark introduces the first miraculous meal.

> [30] When the apostles came back to Jesus, they told him all that they had done and all that they had taught. [31] "Come by yourselves privately to some isolated spot," he said, "and rest for a while"—for there were so many people coming and going that they had not even had time to eat. [32] So they set off privately in their boat for a lonely spot. [33] Many people saw them going, and recognized them, and from all the towns they flocked together to the place on foot and got there before them. [34] On getting out of the boat, Jesus saw a great crowd, and his heart was moved at the sight of them, because they were like sheep without a shepherd; and he began to teach them many things.
> Mark 6:30–34

Verse 30 refers to the disciples as "apostles" or "envoys." They were going to become apostles when the resurrected Christ ordered them to preach the Gospel to all the nations. The use of that title in a pre-Easter context is justified by the fact that Jesus had sent them on a mission right before the first miraculous meal. When they returned from that mission, they reported to Jesus. "They told him all they had done." There is here a clear connection between the mission of the twelve (Mark 6:6b-13) and the first miraculous meal. Those two events follow one another, and, as we shall see, this was not a coincidence.

Verse 33 is particularly weak. It says that "Many saw them going by boat and recognized where they were going." Did Jesus have a retreat house on the other side of the lake where he was known to go on vacation?

We are told that those who saw him leave came from all the towns in Galilee. How could those who lived far from the lake have seen him run away from the crowd? How could they have arrived there before him?

Link between the disciples' mission and the first collective meal

As I said, verse 30 links the first miraculous meal with the return of the disciples from a special mission. Let's read about their mission.

> [7]He called the Twelve to him, and began to send them out as his messengers, two and two, and gave them authority over foul spirits. [8]He instructed them to take nothing but a staff for the journey—not even bread, or a bag, or coins in their purse; [9]but they were to wear sandals, and not to put on a second coat. [10]"Whenever you go to stay at a house," he said, "remain there until you leave that place; [11]and if a place does not welcome you, or listen to you, as you go out of it shake off the dust that is on the soles of your feet, as a protest against them." [12]So they set out, and proclaimed the need of repentance. [13]They drove out many demons, and anointed with oil many who were infirm, and cured them.
>
> Mark 6:7-13

This text is full of anachronisms. The nature of their mission is highly contaminated by their post-Easter activities. Jesus never used oil to heal the sick. This practice was introduced after his death.

Verse 8 is contaminated by instructions to missionaries who were sent to preach the Gospel after the death of Jesus.

Part Two—What happened during the life of Jesus.

All these clues suggest that the nature of the mission was transformed after the death of Jesus.

The fact remains that the first collective meal took place right after the disciples had returned from their mission. This connection is significant. The nature of their mission must have been to invite the people to a rally. Jesus had something important to introduce. So, on the appointed day, Jesus went by boat with his disciples to the appointed place. The people were waiting for them; they had come with plenty of food for the entire day.

If this is what happened, it becomes clear that the disciples' memory of that event was altered most likely after Jesus' death. And the Jesus who treats them so harshly must be the slain Jesus who haunted them and accused them of having betrayed his memory by transforming organized meals into improvised miracles.

So far so good. But why did the memory of what happened on those two occasions have to be repressed? Why did they transform organized meals into miraculous meals? What were they trying to hide in this way? The secret is in the long speech that Jesus made before the first meal. Unfortunately, the text does not mention a single word of what he said on that day. I would say that the text hides what it knows. It is as if it had to mislead us. This could be the case if what Jesus said on that day had become anathema to the Easter faith of the disciples.

Imagine, if you want, the following scenario. The disciples' faith in the resurrection was based on a powerful spiritual experience. That experience was so overwhelming that it became normative. This means that everything else had to be subordinated to it and its theological implications. Now if, during the life of Jesus, something happened that rendered the Easter faith impossible, that event would have had to be removed from their memory. It would have had to be repressed.

This is, if you want, the guiding theory through which I make sense of our two enigmatic texts. Both recognize that there was something wrong with the two meals as reported in the Gospel of Mark. The meals are reported as improvised miracles. If this is what is wrong, then the other alternative is that they were organized, and no miracle had occurred.

A word about the return of the repressed

The repressed returns not overtly but covertly. Their return takes the form of clues that are not easy to recognize. Those clues confirm what has been repressed. Now what was repressed is the long speech that Jesus gave when he introduced the new ritual. The text says this about that speech.

> ³⁴As he went ashore, he saw a great crowd; and he had compassion for them, because they were like sheep without a shepherd; and he began to teach them many things.
> Mark 6:34

In this case, the text hides[3] something important. It hides what Jesus had to say about the new ritual of the meal that he was introducing. All it says is that he spoke for a long time and had to be told to cut it short.

The second element that hides the truth is that the meal was presented as an improvised miracle, not as organized ritual (a ritual that was supposed to be repeated, whence the second collective meal).

The third element that is hidden is that the new ritual was to replace the Passover meal and its sacrificial nature. This would have rendered the Temple sacrifices obsolete.

These are the three elements that were repressed. The meals were transformed into improvised miracles. But what was repressed came back. It took the form of our enigmatic texts. In them the disciples recognized that they had to change the stories for uncontrollable reasons. This is what the hardening of their hearts meant. They had no choice but to do what they did. In the

---

3. I am borrowing this way of speaking from Michel de Certeau. He uses it in his discussion of the texts that were written by mystics. Now the disciples became mystics on account of their resurrection experience. To the extent Mark's narrative reproduces the testimony of a disciple, it bears the marks of that experience.

Part Two—What happened during the life of Jesus.

second enigmatic text, Jesus treats them very harshly. He accuses them of having betrayed his memory. The text misleads us when it claims that those exchanges took place during the life of Jesus and right after the second meal. In reality, the Jesus who criticizes them is the slain Jesus. He haunted them for having betrayed his memory and the memory of what he had introduced on that day.

*

Modern scholarship and Mark's enigmatic text

In his commentary on the Gospel of Mark[4], Camille Focant says that the commentators do not take the risk of proposing an interpretation to Mark's enigmatic text in 8:17–21. Focant has the courage to recognize that nobody knows what it means.

This reminds me of a similar problem concerning the Ninth Amendment to the Constitution. When Judge Bork was nominated to the Supreme Court, he lost the nomination because he had the courage to maintain that the text of the Ninth Amendment was obscure and that we don't know what it means. Consequently, it cannot be used by jurists. Here is what he said, "I do not think you can use the ninth amendment unless you know something of what it means."[5] Those who claim that an enigmatic text is not enigmatic are bound to run into problems.

*

---

4. Camille Focant, *L'évangile selon Marc*, Cerf, Paris, 2010, 307.

5. Quoted by Kurt T. Lash in his book, *The Lost History of the Ninth Amendment*, Oxford University Press, 2009, 11.

Repressed Memories in the Gospel of Mark

Three spiritual phases in the life of Jesus

Phase 1

Jesus heard about John the Baptist and joined his movement. He was baptized "for the forgiveness of his sins" like all the followers of John. At that point, nothing distinguished him from the disciples of John.

Phase 2

When John was arrested, Jesus started his own movement. He recruited some of John's disciples and then he went back to his native Galilee. His message concentrated on the imminent coming of the Kingdom of God. He told the people to repent and believe in what God was going to do.

Phase 3

Jesus was at the height of his popularity in Galilee. Thousands of people would come to his rallies. This is when God revealed something new to him. The coming of the Kingdom of God will mark a new era that will be associated with the end time. In the end time, there is no need for the Temple and its sacrifices. Many prophets had said before him that God does not need sacrifices, but repenting hearts. According to Jesus, this will become the norm in the end time. So, he declared the Temple sacrifices obsolete, and replaced the Passover meal with a non-sacrificial meal that could be celebrated anywhere in the world. The new ritual that he introduced consisted of two parts. The first part was a liturgy of the word. This is when Jesus explained what he was doing (he spoke for a long time according to Mark 6:34). The second part was the liturgy of the meal—a convivial meal where the people shared what they had.

> Note. The Christian ritual that is known as mass, consists of two parts. The first one is a liturgy of the word, and the

Part Two—What happened during the life of Jesus.

second part a liturgy of the meal. But the similarity ends here. The meal ritual that was introduced by Jesus had nothing to do with his body and blood. The Gospel of John made that connection; Jesus did not. His death had nothing to do with the new ritual.

The new ritual was meant to be repeated. As a matter of fact, it was repeated, but only once. Something happened the second time around. The people would not go back home after the second meal. The text says that they remained there for three days. What was going on? The text does not say. But we are lucky in this case. The Gospel of John reveals what was repressed in the Gospel of Mark. It says that the people recognized in Jesus another Moses and wanted to make him king. But he rejected the idea and lost his popularity. Here is John's text,

> When Jesus realized that they were about to come and take him by force to make him king, he withdrew again to the mountain by himself.
> John 6:15

Jesus was left with the twelve and a few others.

> So, Jesus asked the twelve, "Do you also wish to go away?"
> John 6:67

Having lost his popularity in Galilee, Jesus had no other choice but act alone. He will go up to Jerusalem, enter the Temple, and proclaim what God had revealed to him about the end time and the end of Temple sacrifices.

Memories that were repressed by some were not repressed by others. The disciples who abandoned Jesus, because he would not let them proclaim him king did not have to repress the memory of that event. Many years later, John had access to that memory, and he did not have any reason for rejecting it. The source of Mark, on the other hand, had to repress the memory of what Jesus did in Galilee and what he proclaimed in the Temple. Jesus must have been arrested and condemned because he was seen as a lunatic who claims to have special revelations from God that were radically incompatible with Judaism. In other words, Jesus was guilty as charged. He could not be the innocent Lamb of God whose death redeemed the world. This is why the source of Mark had to repress all the memories that contradicted the Easter faith in Jesus Christ, Son of God.

This interpretation of what Jesus had in mind when he went up to Jerusalem is controversial. It is based to a great extent on what the disciples admitted concerning what took place in the Temple. They pleaded guilty to the lesser charge of criticizing the commercial activities that took place in the Temple. The problem is that disturbing the peace is not a capital crime. In his narrative of the trial, Mark says that Jesus was found deserving death by all the member of the Jewish council. This means that he was found guilty of a much more serious charge. Traces of that charge can be found in the "false" testimonies that were made during the trial. The witnesses spoke of a destruction of the Temple. There is here a partial truth. The whole truth was repressed because it would have shown that the death sentence was justified. In this case, Jesus would have been guilty as charged, and he could not have been the innocent Lamb of God whose death was redemptive. This is why I assume that he declared in the Temple that the end time is here and that there is no longer any need for the Temple and its sacrifices.

Part Two—What happened during the life of Jesus.

Who was the source of Mark?

In the enigmatic texts that I have identified in the Gospel of Mark, the disciples are addressed as a group, and they react as a group. Nobody is mentioned by name.

The source of Mark must have spoken in this way. He must have identified with the group and acted as its spokesman. In this way he managed to remain anonymous. Now we know that in the Gospel of Mark, Peter is the one who speaks in the name of the group (See Mark 8:27-30). This is his signature. Therefore, Peter must be the source of Mark. This point is confirmed by John. When Jesus asked the disciples if they wanted to leave him, Peter is the one who answered for the entire group, "We don't have a better alternative" (See John 6:67).

William Wrede discussed this possibility that was based on what Papias[6] said. Here is what he wrote about this point in his introduction (page 9).

> I am leaving completely open the question of the relationship of the Gospel of Mark to Peter. In an investigation of the kind we are undertaking the intrusion of such problems could only have a harmful effect. Everything to do with the internal circumstances of the Gospel must first be explored on its own account. Only afterwards can we ask whether the result favours the tradition of a Petrine basis for the Gospel or not.

Wrede never returns to this question in his book. This suggests that he did not find anything in Mark's narrative that could corroborate the testimony of Papias as reproduced by Eusebius.

In 1901, Freud had not elaborated his study of repressed memories and return of the repressed. Wrede had no way of using it. Instead of psychoanalysis, gospel scholars of his time sought some insights in psychology. Wrede discussed this point in his

---

6. Papias was bishop of Hierapolis in the early First Century. He said that Mark's account is based on the testimony of Peter. His book was lost. Only fragments survived in the writings of Eusebius.

introduction (pages 6–7). He was very reluctant to rely on psychological speculation.

Today we know that repressed memories and the return of the repressed affect individuals who find themselves in conflicting situations. When they are confronted with two contradictory things, and when one takes precedence over the other, they repress the less important one in order to preserve the most important one.

In the Gospel of Mark, there are traces of repressed memories. Those memories refer to a few things that happened during the life of Jesus. I was able to identify some of them thanks to the return of the repressed. As I said before, those memories had to be repressed because they rendered the Christian faith impossible. Mark had no way of knowing anything about repressed memories. He just reproduced Peter's oral recollections as faithfully as he could. In other words, the one whose mind was disturbed was not Mark but Peter.

Conclusion

When he lost his popularity in Galilee, Jesus didn't give up. He decided to go up to Jerusalem and proclaim what was revealed to him. God was going to rule over Israel as in the days of Moses. This new event will mark the beginning of the end time. The Temple and its sacrifices will become obsolete. The Passover meal will be replaced with a non-sacrificial meal. Views of this nature were very dangerous. The disciples knew that. But they decided to go up to Jerusalem and die with him. Here is how their mood is described as they were on the way up to Jerusalem.

> They were on the road, going up to Jerusalem, and Jesus was walking ahead of them; they were amazed, and those who followed were afraid.
> Mark 10:32

They knew what Jesus was going to do in Jerusalem. He was going to proclaim in the Temple what he had proclaimed in

Part Two—What happened during the life of Jesus.

Galilee, when he introduced the first sacred meal. Tragic end of a great prophet!

Jesus did not go up to Jerusalem in a direct line. He made a big detour. First, he went to the Jordan River, to the spot where John was baptizing and where he was baptized. This was a form of pilgrimage to the place where he first heard the call of God. This was his way of revitalizing his resolve and affronting the Jewish establishment in Jerusalem. His tragic death should have signified the end and the failure of his mission. But the resurrection experience of his disciples transformed this failure into a stunning triumph. As he was dyeing on the cross, he thought that God had forsaken him (see Mark 15:34). The resurrection experience reversed this situation. God vindicated him after his death. The question remains, however, whether the disciples' resurrection experience was any different from Jesus' belief in what was revealed to him in the third phase of his life.

*

Reconstruction of what happened in the third phase of Jesus' life

In the last phase of his life, Jesus had a new insight about God's plans for Israel. God was going to rule over Israel as in the days of Moses. The end time will take the form of a return to the beginning[7]. The Temple sacrifices will become obsolete, and the Passover meal will be performed anywhere in the world.

In order to inform his followers of this new development, Jesus organized big rallies with the help of the twelve.

---

7. The beginning can be either the historical beginning with Moses, or the mythical beginning of creation.

Repressed Memories in the Gospel of Mark

What is said and what is not said

We know from the Gospel of Mark that Jesus began with a long speech. He must have introduced what was revealed to him and the reason why he had organized the collective meal. Mark mentions that long speech but fails to say anything about what Jesus had to say.

John, on the other hand, invented Jesus' famous speech in the synagogue of Capernaum. For him, Jesus instituted the Eucharist on that day. This is why he rejects Mark's version in which Jesus instituted the Eucharist during the Last Supper. Unfortunately, the Eucharist as we know it today anticipates the sacrificial death of Jesus and the understanding of the Pascal event. It could not have been anticipated in the pre-Pascal context as John states. Even Mark's version of the Last Supper anticipates in the pre-Pascal context what belongs in the post-Pascal context. Before the death of Jesus, the disciples knew nothing about his post-Pascal identity and what was going to become the Eucharist[8].

The two collective meals had a connection with the Passover meal, not with the Christian Eucharist that did not exist yet. They were to replace, in Jesus' mind, the Passover meal. The Passover meal was sacrificial. It was to be replaced by non-sacrificial meals. This idea of Jesus rendered the Temple sacrifices obsolete. More importantly, it implicitly rejected all sacrifices, including the alleged sacrificial death of the Lamb of God.

A question remains that needs clarification. The connection between the two collective meals and Passover is not made in the Gospel of Mark. I would say that it was repressed. John explicitly says that Passover was near and that the people sat on the green grass. Mark mentions only the second point. He does not quote a word of what Jesus had to say before the meal. In that long speech, Jesus must have mentioned the Passover meal that his new collective meals were supposed to replace in the new divine plan.

---

8. Here we have to be logical. Anything that anticipates the Easter revelation in the pre-Easter context is not historical. This will become clear as my discussion of Mark's narrative progresses.

Part Two—What happened during the life of Jesus.

There is in Mark a remote allusion to the desert and to what Moses did in the desert. He says that the people met in a "deserted" place. The obvious meaning is that it was an isolated place. But the Greek text uses the words éremon *topon* (deserted place) in Mark 6:32 and éremos *ho topos* in verse 35. There is here a vague reference to what happened in the desert during the days of Moses. This is how John understood the allusion, when he says that the people recognized in Jesus a new Moses ("the prophet who is to come into the world") and wanted to make him king. Based on that connection, John compares what Jesus did when he fed the multitude in a deserted place to what God did in the days of Moses, when he gave the starving people manna from heaven. But John went too far when he anticipated the Pascal mystery and the Eucharist, in which the body of Jesus is food and his blood is drink.

The connection with Moses and what happened in the Sinai Desert is not explicitly mentioned by Mark. The organized meals were transformed into improvised miracles. Perhaps John did not know that. Perhaps he did but chose to ignore it for theological reasons. The real reason why the people and the twelve wanted to make him king must have been because Jesus received revelations from God, like Moses, and was empowered to replace the Passover meal with a non-sacrificial meal. This revolutionary revelation called for drastic action.

When Jesus lost his popularity in Galilee, he became depressed. He had to act alone. He had to go up to Jerusalem and proclaim what God had revealed to him.

Now, if he just wanted to introduce convivial meals that had nothing to do with Passover, he would not have been arrested. But if the convivial meals were to replace the Passover meal, and if he declared the Temple sacrifices obsolete, he was in deep trouble.

This is how I would reconstruct what happened.

John says that Jesus spoke of the Temple's destruction, and that he was speaking of his body. But this anticipates the Pascal revelation in a pre-Pascal context. Things become very different if he had declared that God has revealed to him that the Temple sacrifices have become obsolete, and the Passover meal was to be replaced with a non-sacrificial meal. This would have amounted to a moral destruction of the Temple.

In other words, there must have been a direct connection between what Jesus said in the Temple and his death sentence. He was seen as a lunatic who had dangerous revelations and had to be eliminated. All the members of the Jewish council agreed. He deserved to die. He was guilty as charged. In other words, his condemnation was perfectly legal and justified.

After their resurrection experience, the disciples came to the conclusion that his death was sacrificial and redemptive. In order to be able to say so, they had to repress the memory of what happened in Galilee that was repeated in Jerusalem. This is how they repressed the memory of the non-sacrificial meal that was introduced by Jesus on the green shores of the lake. They transformed it into an improvised miracle.

Changing a story can be compared to a forgery. Now a forgery can convince unsuspecting believers. It cannot survive a thorough investigation. Sooner or later, a forgery is bound to be exposed. This is so because, as Freud puts it, a forgery does not fail to leave traces. Once those traces are recognized, the forgery is exposed. In other words, you cannot change a text or a story without running into trouble. Now a forgery can remain unnoticed for centuries as is the case here. For two thousand years, the disciples' forgery remained unrecognized. It is true that some scholars are now saying that the two miraculous meals are unhistorical. But this is still an opinion that is not shared by many conservative scholars. Besides, this is an incorrect view. The two meals did take place on the shores of the lake. But there was nothing miraculous about them.

Certain events are so central to the story of Jesus that they could not be repressed completely. They were repressed by being transformed. Thus, the mission of the disciples was transformed in such a way as to hide any connection with the two miraculous meals. And the two organized meals were transformed into miraculous meals. The disciples' memory was altered unconsciously. So, they were innocent on the conscious level. But in the depth of their subconscious, they knew that they had tampered with the

Part Two—What happened during the life of Jesus.

evidence. Deep down they knew that they had betrayed the memory of Jesus. The Jesus who accuses them of inability to understand and remember is not the historical Jesus. The memories that they had repressed when they became witnesses to the resurrection returned and haunted them.

*

What did Jesus do in the Temple?

According to Mark, he disrupted the commercial activities that were taking place in the Temple. The problem with this recognition is that it is not enough to justify a death sentence. John, on the other hand, is the only one who speaks of the destruction of the Temple. He does not speak of physical destruction. But when he says that Jesus was speaking of his body, he introduces his own interpretation.

But if Jesus proclaimed in the Temple what he had proclaimed in Galilee, namely what God had recently revealed to him, and if that new revelation replaced the Passover meal with a non-sacrificial meal, this would have amounted to putting the Temple out of business. Acting in this fashion would have amounted to transforming Judaism in radical ways. This was absolutely unacceptable. Jesus sounded like a deranged lunatic. He had to be eliminated.

In the end, Jesus failed twice; first in Galilee and next in Jerusalem. But this dual failure that culminated on the cross was transformed into a formidable triumph when his disciples came to the conclusion that God resurrected him and made him Lord and Messiah. That conclusion was based on a powerful and very real resurrection experience.

The Passion Narratives

The Passion narratives (Mark 14 and 15—John 18 and 19) are pious fiction. They see Jesus as the Christ of the faith in a pre-Pascal context.

Jesus must have been arrested in the Temple, tried and executed without delay.

*

Part Two—What happened during the life of Jesus.

We remember the past the way we wish it to be.
The disciples of Jesus did just that.
Our present determines the way we see the past.

*

Degrees of certainty in my reconstruction of what must have happened in Galilee and Jerusalem

*

1—The two collective meals were organized, not improvised.

I would assign a great deal of certainty to this point. The two enigmatic texts that are found in Mark's narrative refer to those two meals and imply that there is something wrong with the way they were narrated. Here we have to play detectives and look for what was wrong with the narrative. The fact that the meals took place cannot be doubted. The second enigmatic text says so openly when it has the disciples confirm what pertains to the leftovers. This leaves us with only one possibility, the meals were organized, and no miracles were performed. My discussion of this possibility was rather interesting. I said that Jesus must have organized them with the help of his disciples. To be sure, there is a connection between the mission of the twelve, as reported by Mark, and the first collective meal. At the same time, it is clear that an attempt was made to hide this connection. In other words, the text plays hide-and-seek with the reader.

2—There were two meals, not just one.

The second meal is not a literary duplicate of the first one. If Jesus introduced a new ritual, that ritual must have been meant to be repeated. The ritual was repeated only once because Jesus lost his popularity right after the second meal. According to Mark, the second encounter lasted for three days (8:2). This means that the people did not go back home right after the second meal. They wanted to make Jesus a king, but he refused. So, they were discussing the possibility of taking him by force and crowning him (John 6:14–15).

Part Two—What happened during the life of Jesus.

3—Jesus lost his popularity

The fact that Jesus lost his popularity after the second meal is confirmed by Mark, not directly, but in a way that has remained unrecognized to this day. The memory of that important event was repressed in the Markan narrative. But what was repressed returned in a subtle way. It returned in a totally different context, that of the parable of the sower. In that context, we are told that the large crowds were excluded from the explanation of the parables and were characterized as "those who are outside." This is a reference to the large number of followers that abandoned Jesus after the second meal.

In this case, Mark confirms what John says about the disciples who abandoned Jesus. But this is not done overtly. To this day nobody that I know of has recognized the connection between Mark 4:10–12 and John 6:66.

Note on the four canonical gospels

Although very different in many respects, they have one thing in common. They are theologically correct. They share the same faith in Jesus Christ, Son of God. Now the Gospel of Mark is very different from the Gospel of John in many ways. To see in the gospel of John revelations that are repressed in Mark can be rejected as naïve on the part of historians. But, if theology is the deciding factor, our four gospels become identical in substance, while remaining different in form. Historians have here a problem. How can two accounts that are so different in form be identical in substance? This discrepancy is due to the nature of the Christian faith. It is based on an event that is unverifiable and that is not of this world. It belongs in the other world, the world of visions and dream—the world of the subconscious. Perhaps historians, that is to say most ordinary historians, should disqualify themselves from the study of the Christian religion. They should stick with the rational world of Kant and steer away from the sub-rational world of Freud.

Jesus used parables in his spiritual discourse, and John used fictional stories such as the "signs" stories, the conversations between Jesus and Nicodemus, or the Samaritan woman in order to express his theological understanding of the Christian mystery.

Religion distinguishes between this world and the other world. Freud distinguishes between the conscious dimension of the mind and its subconscious. I think that the best approach for the study of Christianity is to see it as the product of mysticism as Michel de Certeau discussed it in his *Mystic Fable*.

All the gospel writers were believers and said their faith in Jesus and what they knew about him without intending to falsify anything[9]. But they were not robots. They just did not know that the disciples and eyewitnesses had to repress important memories and transform the historical Jesus so that he would be one and the same as the resurrected Christ. Because the faith in the resurrection had the effect of an atomic bomb on the historical past, what we find in the gospels is not the original landscape but the radically altered one. This means that we have to read the gospels intelligently. Yes, there are many things that are not historical. But they are there for a compelling reason.

What John says about Jesus' rejection of the Messianic crown and his loss of popularity is not contaminated by the atomic bomb. Therefore, it must be reliable. What he says about the Eucharist is contaminated. My reconstruction of what must have happened takes into account those two points. This makes the historians' criteria of authenticity highly unreliable and irrelevant when the gospel is concerned. The burial by Joseph of Arimathea illustrates this point. It is attested by all four gospels and yet it is a pious forgery.

---

9. This is how Papias speaks of what Peter transmitted to Mark. Peter reminisced, and his reminiscences were true. What Papias had no way of knowing is that Peter was also a nervous wreck and suffered of severe mental problems that were caused by his resurrection experience. An atomic bomb exploded inside his mind. He never recovered from that explosion.

Part Two—What happened during the life of Jesus.

4—Reconstruction of what Jesus had to say when he introduced the first collective meal

Mark says that Jesus talked for a long time, but he does not mention a word of what he said on that occasion. He must have explained why he was introducing the new ritual. I cannot say more with any certainty.

What Jesus did during the performance of the ritual is significant. He could have said grace as before any ordinary meal. Perhaps this is what the text wants us to believe. But the text can be interpreted otherwise. Here it is.

> Taking the five loaves and the two fish, he looked up to heaven, and blessed and broke the loaves and gave them to his disciples to set before the people; and he divided the two fish among them all.
> Mark 6:41

This description of what Jesus did strikes me as a religious act. But so is also the blessing of an ordinary meal. What is in favor of a religious ritual is that Jesus could have hardly gone through the trouble of organizing this huge rally just for an ordinary meal.

There is also an analogy between what took place in Galilee and the Christian ritual known as the mass. The Christian ritual consists of two parts, a liturgy of the word and a liturgy of the meal. Now what took place in Galilee follows this pattern. First Jesus spoke for a long time. He must have explained the significance of the meal that followed.

Another reason justifies this interpretation. If all that happened then was an organized meal, the disciples would have had no reason to change that meal into a miraculous one. In this case, nothing would have become incompatible with their post-Pascal faith, and they would not have needed to hide what Jesus said in his long speech. The fact that they have tampered with the facts and repressed the memory of what Jesus said on that day signifies that what happened then became radically incompatible with their post-Pascal faith.

All this confirms my idea that Jesus organized that big rally to introduce something new, most likely something that was revealed to him recently. Let's not forget that Jesus was a prophet and that his new message must have been received from above.

5—Why did the people want to make him king?

John claims that this was on account of the miracle that he had performed. But this explanation cannot be true if the meal was organized, and the people had come with plenty of food for the day. We must look for another reason.

Jesus could have explained that, according to the new revelation that he had received, the new ritual was to replace the Passover ritual. The big difference between those two rituals is that the new ritual could be celebrated away from Jerusalem and did not require any sacrificial offering made in the Temple. Therefore, the Galileans did not have to go up to Jerusalem anymore. In those days the Galileans were second class citizens in Israel. The new revelation gave them the possibility of proclaiming their independence. All they had to do is crown Jesus and declare their independence from Jerusalem. This would have taken the form of a religious schism.

This was not what Jesus had in mind. The new revelation that he had received concerned the Temple sacrifices and Passover specifically. The Temple sacrifices had become obsolete. Consequently, the Passover meal had to be transformed.

6—Connection between the two meals and Passover

In the narrative of the miraculous meal, John is the only one who mentions that Passover was near, and that the grass was green. Mark only mentions that the grass was green, which means that the time was early spring, and that Passover was near.

John takes one more step and connects the new ritual with what happened in the desert during the days of Moses. Then he mentions the Christian Eucharist, in which Jesus' body is food and his blood is drink. Here John seems to suggest that the Eucharist was instituted in Galilee, not during the Last Supper. And to be sure, in John's narrative Jesus does not institute the Eucharist during the Last Supper. He just washed the feet of the disciples.

I said that the new ritual was meant to replace the Passover ritual. This is how I reason here. If the new ritual had nothing to do with Passover, and if it was meant to coexist with Passover, how are we to explain the reaction of his supporters who wanted to make him king? The introduction of an ordinary convivial meal had nothing revolutionary. It could not have justified the movement that wanted to make him king. On the other hand, if Jesus had explained, in his introductory speech (Mark 6:34), that, according to the new revelation that he had received from God, the Temple sacrifices had become obsolete and that the Passover meal had to be replaced with a non-sacrificial meal, then he would have acted as a new Moses, "the prophet who has to come into the world" (John 6:14). In other words, as the new Moses, Jesus' mission was to introduce a new era in the history of Israel. The end time was there. Radical change was to be expected.

What I am saying here is confirmed by what Jesus was accused of. He spoke, we are told, of destroying the Temple. As a matter of fact, proclaiming the Temple sacrifices obsolete was tantamount to a moral destruction of the Temple. This explains his immediate arrest and perfectly lawful condemnation.

7—Mark's two enigmatic texts belong in the post-Pascal logic

Those enigmatic texts (Mark 6:52 and 8:17–21) are misleading. They want us to believe that the disciples' hardening of the heart and inability to understand something important related to the two collective meals took place right after those meals. The second enigmatic text takes one more step and wants us to believe that the Jesus who accuses the disciples of inability to understand and remember was the historical Jesus. If we let the texts mislead us, we won't have a way of interpreting them correctly.

In order to interpret them correctly we must decide whether they express something that took place during the life of Jesus or after his death. Here is a simple way of doing so. Is the context in which those enigmatic texts appear pre-Pascal or post-Pascal? This question can be easily resolved if we go to the first enigmatic text. That text is embedded in the story of Jesus' walking on the lake. Many gospel scholars see in this story an epiphany. Now epiphany can be defined as a revelation of the post-Pascal identity of Jesus in a pre-Pascal context. Consequently, I would say that the context of the first enigmatic text is post-Pascal.

The second enigmatic text wants us to believe that the Jesus who assaults the disciples and accuses them of not understanding and not remembering is the historical Jesus (pre-Pascal context). But is it possible that they would have forgotten something important that was related to those events just a few days after they had taken place? This suggests to me that their memory problem was not ordinary but extraordinary. Perhaps I should even say, not normal but abnormal. We are not talking here of simple forgetfulness, but of repressed memories. Therefore, I would say that the text is misleading. It hides what it knows. The disciples' problems with the two collective meals did not materialize during the life of Jesus, but after his death.

8—An eyewitness, not Mark.

William Wrede took for granted that all the odd things that are in the Gospel of Mark are his invention. I disagree. The return of the repressed requires an eyewitness' action. Mark was not an eyewitness. Therefore, he could not have repressed any disturbing memories. He must have transmitted what he had received from an eyewitness. That eyewitness must have been highly respectable in the Christian community, and Mark must have reproduced very faithfully what he was told. He had no way of knowing that his source of information, namely Peter, had severe psychopathological problems.

Part Two—What happened during the life of Jesus.

*

Christian memory of the trial

In the Gospel of Mark, the trial ends with the following exchanges between the High Priest and Jesus,

> "Are you the Messiah, the Son of the Blessed One?" Jesus said, "I am; and you will see the Son of Man seated at the right hand of the Power, and coming with the clouds of heaven."
> Mark 14:61b–62

It is clear that the question and the answer are contaminated by the post-Easter faith. They must be discarded as unhistorical. But there is some truth in what the alleged false witnesses said about what Jesus said in the Temple. He spoke of the destruction of the Temple. By declaring the Temple sacrifices obsolete, Jesus rendered the Temple useless. His ideas amounted to a moral destruction of the Temple.

The disciples were prepared to plead guilty for a lesser charge. They reduced what Jesus did in the Temple to causing a disturbance. But, as I said before, this charge does not warrant death. If all the members of the Jewish council agreed that Jesus deserved to die, Jesus must have faced very serious charges such as declaring the Temple sacrifices obsolete and transforming the Passover meal into a non-sacrificial meal that can be celebrated anywhere in the world.

Conclusion

The rationale that is guiding me is simple. The reason that is given in Mark and John for the condemnation of Jesus implies the knowledge of the Pascal mystery in a pre-Pascal context. But this was impossible in a pre-Pascal context. Therefore, we must look for another reason. This takes us back to what happened in the Temple. The memory of what Jesus did there is repressed in Mark and John. This means that the historical truth had become anathema to the Easter faith of the disciples. In other words, what Jesus did proclaim in the Temple must have justified his condemnation. But this was totally unacceptable to the disciples. If Jesus was guilty as charged, he could not have been the Lamb of God that atones for the sins of the world. The entire Christian faith would have collapsed if this historical truth was recognized. Therefore, that truth had to be altered and repressed. Our enigmatic texts represent the return of the repressed.

*

Note on Peter's denial of Jesus and Judas' betrayal of Jesus

First the Jerusalem police did not have to look for Jesus in order to arrest him. He must have been arrested in the Temple. In other words, there was no need for a traitor. Judas must have been vilified after the death of Jesus. Most likely he could not believe in the resurrection and became an outcast.

Peter, on the other hand, had a big problem. He had abandoned Jesus when he was arrested. So did all the male disciples (see Mark 14:50). This means that the story in which Peter denied knowing Jesus is fiction. In it, Peter confesses his guilt of having abandoned Jesus.

Here is another point to consider. Peter's faith in the resurrection forced him to proclaim Jesus Messiah and Son of God. But he could not forget his confrontation with Jesus, when he urged the Master to accept the Messianic crown. Jesus rebuked him very harshly and called him Satan[10]. As far as Jesus was concerned, he did not want to hear anything about a Messianic movement. After the resurrection, however, Peter had to proclaim him Messiah and Son of God. By doing so, he betrayed the memory of the historical Jesus. Because of this, I say that it is not Judas who betrayed

---

10. I will go back to this story at the end of this book.

Part Two—What happened during the life of Jesus.

Jesus, but Peter and the other disciples. The problem was that their faith in the resurrection forced them to betray the memory of Jesus. Quite naturally we find traces of this problem throughout the Gospel of Mark, which is based for the most part on Peter's reminiscences. Peter tried to square the circle. He became like so many mystics a mental case. This is the key for understanding the Gospel of Mark.

*

> A PARADOX
>
> Mark's Gospel is based on
> the testimony of an eyewitness.
> But this is precisely
> what makes it
> terribly unreliable.

Repressed Memories in the Gospel of Mark

Memories that are repressed in Mark not in John

In the Gospel of Mark, important memories are repressed that are related to the miraculous feedings of five and four thousand people. John, on the other hand, had access to those memories and reported them in his own way.

As we have seen, Mark mentions two miraculous feedings of large crowds. John mentions only one miraculous feeding. This is a minor difference between Mark and John. More important differences can be found. John had access to information that is not mentioned in Mark. I can identify, in this quick survey, three points.

1—In his discussion of the miracle of the loaves, in which Jesus fed five thousand people out of a few loaves of bread and some fish, John writes,

> [14]When the people saw the sign that he had done, they began to say, "This is indeed the prophet who is to come into the world."
> [15]When Jesus realized that they were about to come and take him by force to make him king, he withdrew again to the mountain by himself.
> John 6:14–15

This means that Jesus rejected the royal crown. He was not the Messiah (the anointed king, "Christos" in Greek). This contradicts what the Gospel of Mark says about Jesus, that he was the Messiah or Christ (not overtly but secretly).

2—This stunning revelation is followed by another one. Jesus lost his popularity in Galilee. The large crowds that enjoyed listening to him abandoned him. His highly successful action in Galilee came to an abrupt end.

> Many of his disciples turned back and no longer went about with him.
> John 6:66

John explains this massive defection with what Jesus said in the synagogue of Capernaum about eating his flesh and drinking his blood. We know that this famous speech of Jesus is based on

Part Two—What happened during the life of Jesus.

John's understanding of the Eucharist. The real reason why Jesus lost his popularity must have been his rejection of the Messianic crown.

3—A third incident is reported in the Gospel of John right after Jesus lost his popularity.

> ⁶⁷So Jesus asked the twelve, "Do you also wish to go away?"
> ⁶⁸Simon Peter answered him, "Lord to whom can we go? [...]"
> John 6:67–68

Those three incidents are not contaminated by the post-Easter faith. They are likely to be historical, but John sets the second and third incidents in the wrong context (that of the speech on the bread of life). None of them is mentioned in the Gospel of Mark. But, as I said earlier, I find in Mark's narrative a muted reference to the large crowds who defected (see the parable of the sower and the exclusion of those who are outside in Mark 4:10–12).

Mark's narrative confirms the information that is found in John. But in Mark, the memory of Jesus losing his popularity is repressed, therefore it is not mentioned overtly. However, this repressed memory returns in the wrong context of the parables, and at a time when Jesus was still very popular. This makes Mark's reference to the large crowd as those who are outside incomprehensible. In this indirect but very valuable way Mark confirms John's revelation. This means that John's account is reliable and can be used to reconstruct what happened in connection with the collective meals.

*

The two feedings that are mentioned in Mark are associated with two contrary things. They show that Jesus was at the height of his popularity in Galilee. Thousands of people would come and listen to him. But this very success of Jesus backfired. The people wanted to proclaim him king. Jesus did not expect this reaction that was totally unacceptable to him. This is how he lost his popularity. His mission in Galilee ended in failure. From that moment on he turned his attention to Jerusalem. This time, he had to work alone.

Nobody was there to greet him when he arrived in Jerusalem. He went to the Temple and acted alone. He must have said in the Temple what he had said in his long speech before the miraculous meal (see Mark 6:34). What he had said then caused his followers, including the twelve, to want to proclaim him king. When he said the same thing in the Temple, he signed his death sentence.

Unfortunately, John had access to only partial truth concerning the collective meal. He did not know that the collective meals were not improvised miracles but organized rituals. As we have seen, Jesus had organized them with the help of his disciples. He sent them on a special mission. They had to go all over Galilee and invite the people to a big rally. Jesus had something new to introduce. So, on the appointed day, he went with his disciples to the appointed place. As he arrived, five thousand people were waiting for him.

This reconstruction of what must have happened is likely to be rejected by many gospel scholars. It does not use the tools of the trade. It does not follow the historical critical method. This is true. I am using here a totally different method.

For some important reason, the memory of what had really happened in Galilee was repressed in the Gospel of Mark. But what had been repressed returned in disguise and can be spotted in Mark's narrative. So far, we have seen an example of this phenomenon. There is in Mark 4:10–12 a reference to the disciples who defected and became outsiders. There is also a trace of another problem in association with the second collective meal. When the new ritual was repeated a second time, the people would not disperse for three days (see Mark 8:2), which suggests that something was going on. Most likely they were caucusing and discussing the idea of making Jesus a king. When he rejected the idea, they decided to make him king by force. This is when Jesus fled the scene.

*

Mark is not the only one who misleads us by setting something in the wrong context. John does the same thing when he attributes

Part Two—What happened during the life of Jesus.

Jesus' loss of popularity to what he is supposed to have said about eating his flesh and drinking his blood. It is clear that this Eucharistic interpretation is post-Pascal set in a pre-Pascal context[11]. The real reason why Jesus lost his popularity must have been his refusal to take the lead of a Messianic movement.

In John's third text, Jesus asks the twelve if they want to drop out. They must have been actively involved in the movement that wanted to proclaim him king. And now they had to make up their minds. Because they had no better choice, and because they had abandoned everything in order to follow him, they had to stay with him. The phrase with which this incident ends is a Johannine addition, "You have the words of eternal life. We believe and know that you are the Holy One of God." This declaration is reminiscent of what Peter says about Jesus in the Gospel of Mark, "You are the Messiah" (see Mark 8:30).

One last remark. John makes it clear that Jesus' kingdom is not of this world (see John 18:36). Because of this theological view, John can recognize that Jesus rejected a Messianic crown that was of this world. The Gospel of Mark, on the other hand, does not make a similar distinction. It insists that Jesus was the Messiah during his life, but that for some reason he wanted to keep that point secret "before" the resurrection. Therefore, to admit that Jesus rejected the Messianic crown would have contradicted the entire Markan message.

Gospel scholars are impressed by the sharp differences that exist between John and Mark. Those differences are real. But they affect the form not the substance of the message. The substance is theological. John expresses it in the ending of his gospel.

> [30]Jesus did many other signs in the presence of his disciples, which are not written in this book. [31]But these are written so that you may come to believe that Jesus is the Christ, the Son of God, and that through believing you may have life in his name.
> John 20:30–31

---

11. I will discuss this point shortly.

Compare this ending with the way Mark starts his gospel.

Gospel of Jesus Christ, Son of God.
Mark 1:1

The theological message is the same. That is why they were so different from all the other gospels that are classified as apocryphal. Mark and John share the same faith in Jesus Christ, Son of God. But they express that faith in different ways. This explains why John used memories that were repressed in Mark.

What next?

So far, I have shown that the Gospel of John is very precious, because it reveals important things that are not overtly stated in the Gospel of Mark, but only covertly. If we continue this comparative study, we will find that neither Mark nor John is univocal. Both are equivocal. In other words, there is a basic contradiction in what they say about Jesus and in the way they portray him. The contradiction exists not only between the two gospels, but even within each gospel. The contradiction concerns what happened during the life of Jesus and what happened after his death. During his life, Jesus rejected the messianic crown and lost his popularity. After his death, however, the disciples went through the resurrection experience and proclaimed him Messiah and Son of God. Thus, he was made Messiah in spite of himself, and when he was no longer there to restrain the disciples.

*

Pre-Easter and post-Easter

My interpretation of the Gospel of Mark is based on the distinction between what is pre-Easter and post-Easter. The narrative confuses those two levels in a systematic way. Anything that anticipates the post-Easter logic in a pre-Easter context is anachronistic. This means that Jesus knew nothing about what the disciples were

Part Two—What happened during the life of Jesus.

going to experience after his death. Their resurrection experience transformed him in their eyes into the Messiah and Son of God. They believed that his sacrificial death redeemed the world. They became the founders of the Christian religion, and they projected their new faith on their pre-Pascal narrative.

Here is a text by Michel de Certeau in which he discusses the mystical discourse. The Gospel of Mark fits in that description. This suggests that it is connected to the reminiscences of a mystic.

> Psychoanalysis and historiography have two different ways of distributing the space of memory. They think differently about the relation between past and present. The first one recognizes the one in the other, the second one poses the one *next to* the other. Psychoanalysis deals with this relation under the modality of 'imbrication' (the one in the place of the other), of repetition (the one produces the other one under a different form), of equivocation or quid-pro-quo (what is "in the place" of what? There are everywhere masks being exchanged, reversals and ambiguity). Historiography sees this relation under the modality of successive events (the one after the other), of correlation (more or less distant proximity), of effect (the one follows the other) and of disjunction (either this one or the other, but not both of them at the same time).
>
> Thus, two strategies of time confront each other, in spite of the fact that their respective fields of operation deal with similar questions. The agreements and disagreements between those two strategies since Freud (18561939) pinpoint the possibilities and the limitations for renewal that their encounter offers historiography.[12]

The encounter between those two disciplines has not materialized so far. Had it materialized, the study of the gospel would have become much more advanced.

*

---

12. Michel de Certeau, *Heterologies, Discourse on the Other*", translated by Brian Massumi, foreword by Wlad Godzich, University of Minnesota Press, eighth printing 2010, 4. The French text can be found in *Histoire et Psychanalyse, entre science et fiction*, Gallimard, Paris, 1987.87.

Chapter 2

Other manifestations of the dualism between pre- and post-Pascal in Mark's narrative

*

In the gospel of Mark there are what I call two-level stories, in which the pre-Pascal and post-Pascal levels coexist in a way that has not been recognized so far. What pertains to the Messianic secret is another Markan feature. The idea is a post-pascal invention. No demons ever revealed that Jesus was the Messiah. This was a post-Pascal invention by the disciples, or just one of them. We shall see that the said disciples identified with the demons who reveal that Jesus was the Messiah despite his silencing orders. This means that the disciples felt guilty of proclaiming Jesus Messiah after his death, although he had definitely rejected the idea during his life. A third point is that Jesus never predicted his death and resurrection. This too was a pious invention.

*

Part Two—What happened during the life of Jesus.

Because the inventors of the Christian religion were the disciples not Jesus, it is essential to reconstruct the mental processes that guided them when they became witnesses to the resurrection.

As far as the disciples of Jesus are concerned, they went through two very different experiences. Their first experience concerned what happened during the life of Jesus. As eyewitnesses they knew what they had seen with their eyes and heard with their ears concerning the historical Jesus. The second experience concerned what happed to them after the death of Jesus. What happened then is their resurrection experience. This spiritual experience that is intimately linked to their reception of the Holy Spirit revealed to them the "true" identity of Jesus, Messiah and Son of God, whose sacrificial death redeemed the world. Whoever believes in him is saved.

In the pre-Pascal logic, Jesus was God's messenger. He spoke of God's Kingdom, not his. In the post-Pascal logic, he became the central message of the disciples. They sincerely believed that God had resurrected him and that he was now sitting at the right hand of the Father. The Christian faith is based on their post-Pascal experience. This experience had retroactive influences on the way the story of Jesus was remembered and told in our gospels.

I think that the interpretation of a difficult or enigmatic text depends on whether it belongs in the pre-Pascal or post-Pascal logic. As we have seen, this point is crucial for the interpretation of Mark's enigmatic texts (6:52 and 8:17–21). Do they say something that happened during the life of Jesus or something that became evident after his death?

The interpretation of the gospel depends on whether the interpreter believes in some harmonious continuity between the pre-Pascal and post-Pascal events, or in a radical disconnect between them. The evidence that my study provides is in favor of the second position. The Christian faith is based on something that happened to the disciples of Jesus after his death, not on something that happened to the dead body of Jesus.

The Koran says that it appeared to them that he died. I say that it appeared to them that he was resurrected. The Koran reproduces

Other manifestations of the dualism between pre- and post-Pascal

an old theory. My conclusion is based on verifiable evidence that is found in our gospels.

*

Other features of Mark's Gospel

So far I have discussed what happened in the third and last phase of Jesus' life.
Now I propose to go back to the way the second phase of his life has been transformed
under the influence of the Pascal faith.
I will show that Mark was unaware of the fact that Peter, his main source of information,
was a terribly unreliable eyewitness.
He systematically repressed the memory of important events and invented fake facts.
But he also was honest enough to give us clues that reveal what he was forced to do.

1

Two-Layer Stories

Stories in which the pre-Pascal and post-Pascal Layers are clearly recognizable.

2

The Messianic secret, a new interpretation.

Jesus gives the disciples and the demons the same silencing order, but that order is not obeyed.
The solution to this question can be found in section 4.

Part Two—What happened during the life of Jesus.

3

Predictions of the Easter event: death-resurrection

Failed and successful initiations into the Christian mystery

4

Peter says that Jesus is the Messiah and Jesus calls him "Satan"

A reconstruction of what pertains to that event.

*

Other manifestations of the dualism between pre- and post-Pascal

1—Two-Layer Stories

First Story: Jesus as teacher and exorcist

A1—²¹They walked to Capernaum. On the next Sabbath Jesus went into the synagogue and began to teach. ²²The people were amazed at his teaching, for he taught them like one who had authority, and not like the teachers of the Law.

> B—²³Now there was in their synagogue at the time a man under the power of a foul spirit, who called out, ²⁴"What do you want with us, Jesus the Nazarene? Have you come to destroy us? I know who you are—the Holy One of God!" ²⁵But Jesus rebuked the spirit, "Be silent! Come out from him." ²⁶The foul spirit threw the man into a fit, and with a loud cry came out from him.

A2—²⁷They were all so amazed that they kept asking each other, "What is this? What is this, a new kind of teaching? He gives his commands with authority even to the foul spirits, and they obey him!" ²⁸His fame spread at once in all directions, through the whole region of Galilee.

Mark 1:21–28

The story is about two things: the way Jesus teaches (with authority) and the authority he has over the unclean spirits. He expels them with ease. In A1 the people admire the way he teaches. He does not teach like the established authorities. He relies on his personal thinking, not on what is in the textbooks. He would not be satisfied with repeating what the Jewish authorities said. On the contrary, his independence suggests that he would not hesitate to criticize them[1]. This made his teaching new. After the exorcism, the people admire not only the way he teaches but also the

---

[1]. In Ancient Israel, the prophets had the risky task of criticizing the kings. In Jesus' days, there were no kings to criticize. As a prophet, he criticized the Jewish authorities.

Part Two—What happened during the life of Jesus.

authority he has over the demons (A2). In the center (B) we read about a strange thing that took place during the exorcism.

Now I want you to notice a very strange thing. In A2 the people who were present in the synagogue act as if they did not hear the exchanges between Jesus and the demon, and as if they did not hear what the demon revealed about Jesus, when he said, 'I know who you are, the Holy One of God.' The meaning of this revelation is that Jesus is the Messiah. Now this revelation is by far the most important information in the entire story. The fact that the audience did not get it suggests that originally no such revelation was made by the demon. Because of this, I reconstruct the original event as follows:

> A1—Jesus goes to the synagogue and starts teaching. The people admire the way he teaches.
>
> B—When he finished teaching, he cured a man possessed by a demon.
>
> A2—Now the people admire Jesus not only for his teaching, but also for the power he has over the demons.

A second layer was added to this original one in order to show that Jesus was the Messiah of the Christian revelation. The addition was made in the central section B. Originally the demon remained mute. He did not say anything, namely he did not reveal that Jesus was the Messiah, and Jesus did not have to silence him.

William Wrede did not fail to notice that, in this story, those who were present in the synagogue act as if they did not hear what was revealed by the demon about Jesus. He writes, "The demon has cried out the secret of the holy God and according to Mark no one was to hear this" (133). Wrede tends to blame everything on Mark. This prejudice prevented him from seeing the other side of the coin. The people who were in the synagogue and witnessed the exorcism did not mention what the demon had revealed because no such revelation was made at that time. The second layer of the story has all the features of a post-Pascal event. This means that the unclean spirit did not reveal anything about Jesus, and that the second layer was added when the story was told years after

Other manifestations of the dualism between pre- and post-Pascal

Jesus had died. We have here the reverse of repressed memories. Instead of hiding what happened, a new thing is added that never happened. In the same way as repressed memories are to be attributed to disturbed minds, so also the invention of events that never happened must be attributed to a disturbed mind, that is to say a mind that was under the influence of powerful forces (remember what the disciples admitted about the hardening of their hearts in Mark 6:52 and 8:17.

Here is how I would reconstruct what happened in the mind of Peter, the source of Mark. In his reminiscences Peter transformed the original story. He made the demon reveal the Messianic identity of Jesus and had Jesus silence him. This is how his Easter faith transformed retroactively his memory of what had happened in the synagogue of Capernaum.

*

Second text: Jesus cures a paralyzed man.

 A1—¹Some days later, when Jesus came back to Capernaum, the news spread that he was in a house there; ²and so many people collected together, that after a while there was no room for them even around the door; and he began to tell them his message.

 B—³Some people came, bringing to him a paralyzed man, who was being carried by four of them. ⁴They were unable to get him near to Jesus, because of the crowd, so they removed the roof above Jesus, and, when they had made an opening, they let down the mat on which the paralyzed man was lying. ⁵When Jesus saw their faith, he said to the man, "Child, your sins are forgiven." ⁶But some of the teachers of the Law who were sitting there were debating in their minds, ⁷"Why does this man speak like this? He is blaspheming! Who can forgive sins except God?" ⁸Jesus, at once intuitively aware that they

Part Two—What happened during the life of Jesus.

> were debating with themselves in this way, said to them, "Why are you debating in your minds about this? ⁹Which is easier?—to say to the paralyzed man, 'Your sins are forgiven'? Or to say 'Get up, and take up your mat, and walk'? ¹⁰But so you may know that the Son of Man has power to forgive sins on earth"—here he said to the paralyzed man—¹¹"To you I say, Get up, take up your mat, and return to your home." ¹²The man got up, and immediately took up his mat, and went out before them all;
>
> A2—at which they were amazed, and, as they praised God, they said, "We have never seen anything like this!"

Mark 2:1-12

Did you notice what is missing in A2? The people who were in the house witnessed the healing of the paralyzed man and expressed their amazement. But they act as if the entire discussion about remission of sins did not occur. This is very strange, because the revelation concerning Jesus' authority to forgive sins is much more important than his ability to cure sick people. Because of this omission, I reconstruct the original event as follows:

> A1—Jesus teaches to a full house.
>
> B—A paralyzed man is brought in through the roof. Jesus cures him.
>
> A2—The people admire his healing powers.

In other words, Jesus did not say to the young man, "Your sins are forgiven." And no scribes were present in the house, who would have objected to what Jesus had said. The second layer (verses 5 to 10) was added to the story after the resurrection experience. Now we hear Jesus reveal that as 'Son of Man' he has the authority to forgive sins. In this passage, Jesus is introduced for the first time as 'Son of Man,' which is a Messianic title similar to 'Son of God.'

Other manifestations of the dualism between pre- and post-Pascal

What is typical of the second layer in our two stories is that it is used to show that Jesus is the Messiah and that he was so during his earthly life, not overtly but secretly.

What is illustrated in those two stories is typical of the Gospel of Mark as a whole. It, too, consists of two layers, an original one and a superimposed one. The purpose of the second layer is theological, and aims at showing that Jesus was, throughout his earthly life, the Messiah of the Easter revelation. This had become a requirement of the Easter revelation.

The first layer represents what happened during the life of Jesus. Information of this nature must go back to an eyewitness. The second layer was added after the resurrection (by someone who was at the same time an eyewitness of what happened during the life of Jesus and a witness to the resurrection). That disciple was a very bad forger. In the story of the paralyzed man, he says that some scribes were present in the house. This is highly unlikely. The scribes were not disciples of Jesus. They represent the religious establishment. But their presence was needed so that they could object to what Jesus allegedly said about forgiveness of sins. There is always a way of debunking a forgery.

It is hard to believe that Mark had nothing to do with these two-layer stories. But he knew nothing about the disciples' problem, and he could not have put himself in their shoes. He must have reproduced those stories as he had received them. By doing so, he was very precious. Wrede, on the other hand, fell in the trap of attributing everything to Mark and blaming him for "his" inconsistencies. The two-layer stories were invented by someone who had a very serious problem and had to find ways of solving it. He knew that during his life Jesus refused the Messianic crown. He repressed that memory, because, after the death of Jesus, he had to proclaim him Messiah and Son of God. Whence the need to claim that Jesus was so during his life, but that he wished to keep his Messianic identity secret. He did not know that John was going to reveal the fact that Jesus had rejected the Messianic crown and did not want to have anything to do with the Messianic idea. John

Part Two—What happened during the life of Jesus.

could live with this idea, not the disciple who was the source of Mark.

A final note

It is important to understand that the first layers of those two stories did not exist in written form. They existed in the memory of a disciple. When he told those stories, years after the death of Jesus, his memory of the past was altered under the influence of his Easter faith in Jesus Christ, Son of God.

"History is what the present chooses to remember about the past" (Carl Becker, historian). I should add to this that the present decides how the past is to be remembered. This is particularly true about national and religious memory. National and religious myths control the way the past is remembered.

The second-layer stories fall in the category of fake but pious news. Their purpose is to reconcile the historical past with the theological present—what happened during the life of Jesus and what happened to the disciples after his death.

*

Note on miracle workers

In the ancient world, there were people who could heal the sick. They existed in Israel as well as in the pagan world. Even today, we have pilgrimage places where miracles occur (Lourdes in France is a good example). The Bible mentions Elijah and his disciple Elisha. Elijah could outperform his pagan counterparts. But it is important to note that this did not make Elijah and Elisha divine beings. The same was true of Jesus. He was deified after his death not on account of his miracles, but on account of his alleged resurrection. The Gospel of John transformed the miracles into signs[2]

---

2. Most of those signs are pious forgeries. They are invented stories (similar to the parables of the other gospels) that illustrate a theological belief in Jesus

Other manifestations of the dualism between pre- and post-Pascal

that reveal the divine nature of Jesus. Based on this view, most Christians believe that Jesus' miracles prove that he was divine. The other gospels confirm what I am saying here. In his confrontations with the Jewish leadership, Jesus rejected their explanation, that he expelled the demons with the help of their chief demon and insisted that he did so with the help of God (see Mark 3:22–30 and Matthew 12:22–32). The Koran says a similar thing about the miracles of Jesus. He performed them with God's permission not with any divine powers that he had (See Koran 5:116–119).

*

Christ.

Part Two—What happened during the life of Jesus.

2—Jesus as exorcist

There are five passages in the Gospel of Mark where Jesus exorcizes people who were believed to be possessed. The first exorcism takes place in the synagogue of Capernaum. We have read that story, so I will move on to the next passage.

Second text

> 1—³²That evening, at sundown, they brought to him all who were sick or possessed with demons. ³³And the whole city was gathered around the door. ³⁴And he cured many who were sick with various diseases and cast out many demons; and he would not permit the demons to speak, because they knew him.
> Mark 1:32–34

Third text

The third passage is very similar.

> 3—⁷Jesus departed with his disciples to the sea, and a great multitude from Galilee followed him; ⁸hearing all that he was doing, they came to him in great numbers […]. ⁹He told his disciples to have a boat ready for him because of the crowd, so that they would not crush him; ¹⁰for he had cured many, so that all who had diseases pressed upon him to touch him. ¹¹Whenever the unclean spirits saw him, they fell down before him and shouted, "You are the Son of God!" ¹²But he sternly ordered them not to make him known.
> Mark 3:7–12

The first exorcism takes place in the synagogue of Capernaum, where Jesus was teaching. Quite naturally the exorcism is associated with the teaching of Jesus. In the two passages we have just read, the exorcisms are associated with healing the sick. Those two activities (healing and exorcism) are distinguished here because of the strange things that pertain to possession. Possession is a sickness with a twist. It affects the body and the mind. In many ancient cultures sickness was understood as an act of the spirits. If the spirits are displeased, they can cause sickness. That is why the cure ritual took the form of prayer to the spirits, in an effort to soothe them so they will stop tormenting the sick person. When the sickness involved physical convulsions (epilepsy, for example) and signs of madness, it was considered a possession.

In her commentary on the Gospel of Mark, Adela Yarbro Collins shows that exorcisms were practiced in Judaism and paganism.[3] In this respect the gospel is not unique. Even in modern times, we hear about cases of possession requiring exorcism. Michel de Certeau studied a famous case, which took place in the seventeenth century, in the French provincial town of Loudun.[4] The nuns of a monastery became possessed, and the parish priest was held responsible for those possessions. He was found guilty of sorcery and burned alive in 1634.

*

---

3. Adela Yarbro Collins, *Mark, A Commentary*, Fortress press, 2007, 161–173.

4. Michel de Certeau, *The Possession at Loudun*, translated by Michael B. Smith, The University of Chicago Press, 2000.

Part Two—What happened during the life of Jesus.

3—The Messianic Secret

The demons reveal that Jesus is the Messiah, and Jesus silences them. He wants to keep his Messianic identity secret.

Let's examine what the demons do. They do, in a pre-Easter context, what the disciples did in a post-Easter context. What they say about Jesus is theologically correct. This suggests to me that the disciples identified themselves with the demons. Let's examine that possibility.

But first let me say that there are stories in which Jesus silences the disciples as he silenced the demons. Here is a pertinent story.

> ^{32}Some people brought to him a man who was deaf and almost dumb, and they begged Jesus to place his hand on him. ^{33}Jesus took him aside from the crowd in private, put his fingers into the man's ears, and touched his tongue with saliva. ^{34}Then, looking up to heaven, he sighed, and said to the man, "Ephphatha!" which means 'Be opened.' ^{35}The man's ears were opened, the string of his tongue was freed, and he began to talk plainly. ^{36}Jesus insisted on their not telling anyone; but the more he insisted, the more perseveringly they made it known, ^{37}and a profound impression was made on the people. "He has done everything well!" they exclaimed. "He makes even the deaf hear and the dumb speak!"
>
> Mark 7:32–37

Have you noticed what is strange about this story? Jesus dismissed the crowd and acted in private. But after he healed the man "he ordered them" to tell no one. This means that many people were there to witness the miracle. Who could that be? Some of the disciples must have been present. They witnessed the miracle and would not obey the Master's clear order to remain silent.

On two other occasions, Jesus ordered the disciples to keep his Messianic identity secret. When Peter recognized that Jesus is the Messiah (Mark 8: 30) and as Jesus was coming down the Transfiguration mountain, he ordered the three disciples who were with

Other manifestations of the dualism between pre- and post-Pascal

him "to tell no one about what they had seen, until after the Son of Man has risen from the dead" (Mark 9:9).

There is a clear parallelism between the demons and the disciples. This is confirmed by the fact that Peter is called "Satan" by Jesus (see Mark 8:33).

We have seen that, in the first encounter with a man possessed by a demon in the synagogue of Capernaum (Mark 1:21–27) we had a two-level story. The second level in which the demon reveals that Jesus is the Messiah is post-Pascal. And I have concluded that no demons ever revealed that Jesus was the Messiah. Those stories were transformed by the disciples after the resurrection in order to show that Jesus was during his life the Messiah of the Christian religion. In other words, they have lied (not by choice but by a necessity that caused their hardening of the heart) and they identified themselves with the demons.

*

Part Two—What happened during the life of Jesus.

4—Failed Initiations: The Three Predictions of the Passion

*

First prediction

³¹Then he began to teach them that the Son of Man must undergo much suffering, and that he must be rejected by the elders, and the chief priests, and the teachers of the Law, and be put to death, and rise again after three days. ³²He said all this quite openly. But Peter took Jesus aside and began to rebuke him. ³³Jesus, however, turning around and seeing his disciples, rebuked Peter. "Out of my sight, Satan!" he exclaimed. "For you look at things, not as God does, but as people do."
Mark 8:31–33

Second prediction of the Easter event

³⁰Leaving that place, Jesus and his disciples went on their way through Galilee; but he did not wish anyone to know it, ³¹for he was instructing his disciples, and telling them –"The Son of Man is being betrayed into the hands of his fellow men, and they will put him to death, but, when he has been put to death, he will rise again after three days." ³²But the disciples did not understand his meaning and were afraid to question him.
Mark 9:30–32

Third prediction

³²They were on the road going up to Jerusalem, with Jesus walking in front of them. The disciples were filled with awe, while those who were following behind were overwhelmed with fear. Gathering the Twelve around

Other manifestations of the dualism between pre- and post-Pascal

him once more, Jesus began to tell them what was about to happen to him. ³³"Listen!" he said. "We are going up to Jerusalem; and there the Son of Man will be betrayed to the chief priests and the teachers of the Law, and they will condemn him to death, and they will give him up to the Gentiles, ³⁴who will mock him, spit on him, and scourge him, and put him to death; and after three days he will rise again."

Mark 10:32–34

The three predictions of the Passion are initiations that fail. The message does not go through. I shall compare this to two successful initiations. All those initiations take place when the people are on the road, symbol of the spiritual journey.

In the second prediction of the Passion, we are told that Jesus wanted to be alone with his disciples. He wanted to initiate them into the Easter mystery. Quite naturally the initiation took place on a deserted road. This time, however, we are openly told that the disciples did not understand what he was telling them.

In the first prediction of the Passion, we are told that Peter understood what Jesus was talking about, but that he tried to change his somber mood. But this attempt ended in disaster. Peter missed the point and was called Satan.

The third initiation describes the mood of the group as they were going up to Jerusalem. Jesus was walking alone ahead of the group. The disciples followed. The mood was somber. In sharp contrast, a successful initiation produces joy and great satisfaction. Let's compare this to the following successful initiations.

*

Part Two—What happened during the life of Jesus.

5—Successful initiations

1—On the road to Emmaus

The story takes place after the death of Jesus and on the alleged day of the resurrection.

[13] It happened that very day that two of the disciples were going to a village called Emmaus, which was about seven miles from Jerusalem, [14] talking together, as they went, about all that had just taken place. [15] While they were talking about these things and discussing them, Jesus himself came up and went on their way with them; [16] but their eyes were blinded so that they could not recognize him. [17] "What is this that you are saying to each other as you walk along?" Jesus asked. They stopped, with sad looks on their faces, [18] and then one of them, whose name was Cleopas, said to Jesus, "Are you staying by yourself at Jerusalem, that you have not heard of the things that have happened there within the last few days?"

[19] "What things do you mean?" asked Jesus. "Why, about Jesus of Nazareth," they answered, "who, in the eyes of God and all the people, was a prophet, whose power was felt in both his words and actions; [20] and how the chief priests and our leading men gave him up to be sentenced to death, and afterward crucified him. [21] But we were hoping that he was the Destined Deliverer of Israel; yes, and besides all this, it is now three days since these things occurred. [22] And what is more, some of the women among us have greatly astonished us. They went to the tomb at daybreak [23] And, not finding the body of Jesus there, came and told us that they had seen a vision of angels who told them that he was alive. [24] So some of our number went to the tomb and found everything just as the women had said, but they did not see Jesus."

[25] Then Jesus said to them, "Foolish men, slow to grasp all that the prophets have said! [26] Was not the Christ bound to undergo this suffering before entering into his glory?" [27] Then, beginning with Moses and all the prophets, he explained to them all through the scriptures the passages that referred to himself. [28] When they got near

Other manifestations of the dualism between pre- and post-Pascal

the village to which they were walking, Jesus appeared to be going further; ²⁹but they pressed him not to do so. "Stay with us," they said, "for it is getting towards evening, and the sun in already low." So Jesus went in to stay with them. ³⁰After he had taken his place at the table with them, he took the bread and said the blessing, and broke it, and gave it to them. ³¹Then their eyes were opened and they recognized him; but he disappeared from their sight. ³²"How our hearts glowed," the disciples said to each other, "while he was talking to us on the road, and when he explained the scriptures to us!"

³³Then they immediately got up and returned to Jerusalem, where they found the Eleven and their companions all together, ³⁴who told them that the Master had really risen, and had appeared to Simon. ³⁵So they also related what had happened during their walk, and how they had recognized Jesus at the breaking of the bread.

Luke 24:13-35

This story is a very nice piece of literature. It is very well written. I will just identify its main articulations. That this is an initiation scene is clear. The two disciples decided to go back home after the terrible events that culminated in the crucifixion of Jesus. They had heard the news that Jesus had appeared to the women (Luke 24:1-8). But they discarded it as women's talk.

Jesus acts here as the genius who will initiate the two depressed men. A genius is a spirit that comes and goes. It conveys to human beings some insight or some revelation. In Luke's story Jesus is the genius who will initiate the two disciples. Once the initiation is complete, he disappears.

Note that, in this case as in the three initiation attempts found in Mark, Jesus is the agent of the initiation. He failed in three cases and was successful in one case. A comparative study of the various attempts will show why he was bound to fail in the three cases that are reported in Mark. He stated the raw facts (suffering, death, resurrection) without explaining how they fit in the divine plan. The Easter event makes sense only if the raw facts are given their theological meaning.

Part Two—What happened during the life of Jesus.

How could the historical Jesus have made such a mistake? My answer is that, had he really attempted to initiate the disciples during his life, he would not have failed to do what Luke says he has done after the resurrection. The mere fact that the Markan initiations failed proves that the stories are not historical. The likelihood that the historical Jesus did not know anything about the Easter revelation becomes very high.

An initiation attempt is likely to fail if it is conducted 'à froid'—it must be conducted 'à chaud'. In other words, one must beat the iron when it is hot. The initiation must come as an answer to questions or problems that are real. Thus, the disciples of Emmaus[5] just had a powerful and disastrous experience. They had hoped that Jesus would be successful in changing the course of history. But his sudden death left them hurt and disappointed. They were ready to listen to Jesus as he told them how misguided they were. He took the time to introduce them to a new reading of the Scriptures and a new understanding of God's design. He explained to them the theological meaning of what happened. Without theology history remains a series of raw events. Theology is what gives meaning to human existence.

In the initiation scenes, the Jesus of Luke is a good theologian; the Jesus of Mark is a lousy one.

The initiation of the disciples of Emmaus was complete when they recognized Jesus as he broke the bread. They no longer needed him. He could disappear.

The story ends with a complete reversal of their mood. In the beginning, they were depressed. In the end they were elated. Their hearts were burning as they listened to Jesus. They go back to Jerusalem with the good news of their encounter with the resurrected Christ. Before their initiation, they were going back to Emmaus (their past). After their initiation, they reversed their destination. They went back to Jerusalem (their future).

We have in this story all the components of a successful initiation.

---

5. This entire story is pious fiction.

Other manifestations of the dualism between pre- and post-Pascal

*

2—Philip and the Ethiopian

²⁶Meanwhile an angel of the Lord had said to Philip, "Set out on a journey southwards, along the road that runs down from Jerusalem to Gaza." (It is now deserted). ²⁷So Philip set out on a journey; and on his way he came on an official of high rank, in the service of Candace, Queen of the Abyssinians. He was her treasurer, and had been to Jerusalem to worship, ²⁸and was now on his way home, sitting in his carriage and reading the prophet Isaiah.

²⁹The Spirit said to Philip, "Go up to the carriage over there and keep close to it." ³⁰So Philip ran up, and he heard the Abyssinian reading the prophet Isaiah.

"Do you understand what you are reading?" he asked. ³¹"How can I," the other answered, "unless someone will explain it to me?" and he invited Philip to get up and sit by his side. ³²The passage of scripture which he was reading was this –

'Like a sheep, he was led away to slaughter,
   and as a lamb is dumb in the hands of its shearer,
   so he refrains from opening his lips.
³³He was humiliated and justice was denied him.
   Who will tell the story of his generation?
   For his life is cut off from earth.'

³⁴"Now," said the Treasurer, addressing Philip, "tell me, of whom is the prophet speaking? Of himself, or of someone else?" ³⁵Then Philip began, and, taking this passage as his text, told him the good news about Jesus.

³⁶Presently, as they were going along the road, they came to some water, and the Treasurer exclaimed, "Look! Here is water; what is to prevent my being baptized?" ³⁷*Some later manuscripts add: Philip said, "If you believe with your whole heart, you may." And he replied, "I believe that Jesus Christ is the Son of God."³⁸So he ordered the carriage to stop, and they went down into the water—both Philip and the Treasurer—and Philip baptized him. ³⁹But, when they came up out of the water, the

Part Two—What happened during the life of Jesus.

Spirit of the Lord caught Philip away, and the Treasurer saw no more of him; for he continued his journey with a joyful heart. [40]But Philip was found at Ashdod, and, as he went on his way, he told the good news in all the towns through which he passed, until he came to Caesarea.
Acts 8:26–40

This is another initiation story. Philip is the initiation genius here. He is guided by the spirit who tells him where to go and what to do. At the end of the initiation, the spirit makes him disappear.

The Ethiopian official was on his way back home after a pilgrimage to Jerusalem. He was reading a passage from Prophet Isaiah. He did not know who the prophet was talking about in that passage. So, when Philip asked him if he understood it, he asked him to join him and explain it to him.

An initiation must come as an answer to real questions. Those who have questions are open to explanations. They are receptive.

In this story we know the passage the Ethiopian was reading. We do not have any details about the actual explanation of Philip. But it is easy to imagine what that explanation consisted of. Jesus was the suffering servant of God of whom Isaiah was speaking. No objections were made, and no questions were raised. The Ethiopian was baptized and Philip disappeared. The man went on his way full of joy.

*

Back to Mark

"But they did not understand what he was saying and were afraid to ask him."

Their inability to understand is not justified by any alleged obscure statement made by Jesus. But even if his statement had been obscure, all they had to do was ask him to clarify what he said. Why did they not do that? Here we are told that they were afraid to do so.

Fear can be justified or unjustified. In this case, it is unjustified. There is no valid reason for their fear of asking Jesus for an explanation. This suggests that their fear is pathological. Because the fear is unreal, we are to understand that this incident does not belong in the real world but in the dream world of the disciples. Their Easter faith required that Jesus knew what pertains to the Easter mystery of his death and resurrection. So, they invented the predictions of the Passion. But deep in their subconscious they knew that this was not true. This repressed memory came back in the form of the negative statement.

From a psychological point of view, a failed initiation is as good as an initiation that never took place. The end result is the same.

When an eyewitness is compelled to change the facts for religious reasons, he does so, so to speak, under duress. But because his memory of the past has been repressed, he is sincerely convinced he is reporting the historical truth. What happens then is that what has been repressed returns, and takes the form of an obscure negative statement which is the equivalent of a denial of the alleged event.

If we rely on the substance of what is said in the negative statement, we are led to believe that the prediction of the Passion did take place, and that the disciples were too dumb to understand it. But if we rely on the form, we are to conclude that the negative statement denies the historicity of the prediction of the Passion.

Note on form versus substance

When we try to interpret a text, we tend to rely on the substance of what it says. But there are cases where the substance is problematic. This makes any ordinary interpretation very difficult. In those cases, we should rely on the form of the text instead of on its contents. Here is what Michel de Certeau says about this point. He is not speaking of any text, but of texts that are related to a mystical experience.

Part Two—What happened during the life of Jesus.

The document does not *mention* what it *knows*; it hides what organizes it; it unveils solely by its *form* what it erases from its *content*.[6]

*

---

[6]. Michel de Certeau, *The Writing of History*, translated by Tom Conley, Columbia University Press, 1988. 332.

Other manifestations of the dualism between pre- and post-Pascal

6—Peter recognizes that Jesus is the Messiah and Jesus calls him 'Satan'

*

Two connected stories

Peter proclaims that Jesus is the Messiah

[27] Afterward Jesus and his disciples went into the villages around Caesarea Philippi; and on the way he asked his disciples this question—"Who do people say that I am?" [28] "John the Baptist," they answered, "but others say Elijah, while others say one of the prophets." [29] "But you," he asked, "who do you say that I am?" To this Peter replied, "You are the Christ." [30] At which Jesus charged them not to say this about him to anyone.

First prediction of the Passion

[31] Then he began to teach them that the Son of Man must undergo much suffering, and that he must be rejected by the elders, and the chief priests, and the teachers of the Law, and be put to death, and rise again after three days. [32] He said all this quite openly. But Peter took Jesus aside, and began to rebuke him. [33] Jesus, however, turning around and seeing his disciples, rebuked Peter. "Out of my sight, Satan!" he exclaimed. "For you look at things, not as God does, but as people do."

Mark 8:27–33

*

The Messianic identity of Jesus is now openly recognized. The text implies that Jesus agreed with Peter that he was the Messiah.

Part Two—What happened during the life of Jesus.

He just tells the disciples not to tell anyone about his Messianic identity.

Six days later, the Transfiguration took place (see Mark 9:2–13) in which the true identity of Jesus was revealed. The heavenly voice said, "This is my Son." Now the Transfiguration story specifies the following point:

> As they were coming down the mountain, he ordered them (Peter, James and John) to tell no one about what they had seen, until after the Son of Man had risen from the dead."
> Mark 9:9

Mark's message is now clear. The silencing order was only temporary. It was to end after the resurrection. This is what the text wants us to believe.

Peter's profession of faith as a two-level story

In the first level, we hear what the people think about Jesus. Many opinions are listed. In the second level, Peter proclaims that Jesus is the Messiah. The first level is pre-Pascal and the second level is post-Pascal. This means that the second level was added after the death of Jesus. In this particular case, Peter acts as the demon that was expelled in the synagogue of Capernaum (Mark 1:21–28). The demon revealed that Jesus is the Messiah. Jesus, on the other hand, ordered him not to do so. Those two elements are found in Peter's profession of faith. This confirms the fact that the disciples identified with the demons.

*

Literary structure of the two stories 27–30 and 31–33

Here is how our two stories are structured:

Other manifestations of the dualism between pre- and post-Pascal

> A1—Fact: what the people say about Jesus.
> B1—Fiction: what Peter says about Jesus.
> B2—Fiction: first prediction of the Passion/Resurrection
> A2—Fact: Jesus rebukes Peter.

In this *inclusio* two fictional events are preceded and followed by two factual events. The fictional events are post-Pascal; the factual events are pre-Pascal.

*

Why do I maintain that the harsh rebuke of Peter took place?

This violent incident that took place between Jesus and Peter could not have been invented after the resurrection. Therefore, it must be classified as pre-Pascal. But, if it did really happen, it could not have taken place in the context of the first prediction of the Easter mystery. This event is post-Pascal and could not have materialized during the life of Jesus. The confrontation between Jesus and Peter must have happened in a different context. We know that Jesus lost his popularity when he rejected the Messianic crown. What is not said is that there is a relation between the popular desire to make Jesus king and the rebuke of Peter. The twelve disciples must have been at the head of the movement that wanted to make Jesus king. When Jesus rejected the idea Peter must have tried to influence his decision. Opportunities of this nature don't happen every day. It is now the time to act, insisted Peter. That is when Jesus got mad at him and rebuked him so harshly.

This is how I would reconstruct what happened. After Jesus' death, Peter became an idol. He was so highly respected that nobody would have mentioned this incident even if one knew that it was true. Only Peter could have repressed the memory of that event. But the repressed returned in a different context.

Part Two—What happened during the life of Jesus.

Note about the people's opinion about Jesus

I said that what is reported here is factual. As a matter of fact, it reproduces a survey that was mentioned earlier in the Markan narrative. Here is the text.

> [14]Now King Herod heard of Jesus; for his name had become well known. People were saying—"John the Baptizer must have risen from the dead, and that is why these miraculous powers are active in him." [15]Others again said—"He is Elijah," and others—"He is a prophet, like one of the great prophets." [16]But when Herod heard of him, he said—"The man whom I beheaded—John—he must be risen!"
> Mark 6:14-16

In this passage, we have a survey of what the people thought of Jesus. Therefore, Jesus' first question was superfluous. He knew what the people thought of him. The purpose of Jesus' first question is to introduce his second question, "But you, who do you think that I am". Speaking in the name of the group, Peter said, "You are the Messiah."

*

Other manifestations of the dualism between pre- and post-Pascal

Conclusion

In his introduction to the Gospel of Mark, Camille Focant[7] writes:

> Rooted in the way the faith in Jesus was formed, the gospel is marked by a theological undertaking which consists in showing in a narrative that the crucified one and the resurrected one are one and the same (person)."[8]

This is a perceptive reading of the gospel's central concern. Mark's narrative is obsessed with the need to show that the historical Jesus and the Christ of the faith are one and the same person. Focant takes for granted that this was indeed the case. I have argued that this was the message of Mark's overt discourse, but that the covert discourse contradicted it.

Like most theologians and gospel scholars Focant knows nothing about Mark's covert discourse and what it reveals about what happened and did not happen during the life of Jesus. In my study of Mark's narrative, I have shown that the historical Jesus was real, not the resurrected Christ. The faith in the resurrection of Jesus was based on a spiritual experience that affected the disciples but did not affect the dead body of Jesus.

This conclusion was based on the fact that the burial story at the hands of Joseph of Arimathea was pious forgery, and that, therefore, the empty-tomb discovery was part of that forgery. In other words, in order to show that their faith in the resurrection affected the dead body of Jesus, the disciples invented the second burial story and the stories of the empty tomb, all of which are attested by the four gospels but are unhistorical.

In the second part of this book, I centered my attention on Mark's narrative. First, I have introduced Mark's covert discourse, which shows that the two collective meals were organized, not

---

7. Teaches at the Catholic University of Louvain, Belgium.

8. Camille Focant, *L'évangile selon Mark*, Les Éditions du Cerf, Paris, 2010. 30. "Enraciné dans le développement de la foi en Jésus, l'évangile est marqué par un projet théologique : faire apparaître dans un récit l'identité entre le crucifié et le ressuscité, l'identité entre Jésus de Nazareth et le Christ vivant au sein des communautés chrétiennes primitives."

Part Two—What happened during the life of Jesus.

improvised, and that Jesus organized them with the help of his disciples. He had received new revelations concerning God's plan for Israel. According to those plans, something was going to affect the Temple and the Passover ritual. The Temple sacrifices were going to become obsolete, and Passover will be celebrated anywhere in the world, not just in Jerusalem. This interpretation of what Jesus had in mind remains controversial, because I don't have any positive evidence confirming it. But it explains why Jesus was lawfully and unanimously condemned to death by all the members of the Jewish Council.

In the second part of Part 2, I have shown how the Markan narrative has transformed the historical Jesus under the influence of the pascal faith. In other words, I did what Focant does not do in his reading of Mark. I show how Mark's narrative has transformed the historical Jesus and made him identical with the resurrected Christ.

Focant was not aware of the fact that Peter was Mark's source of information concerning the historical past, and that Peter had severe psychopathological problems that affected his memory of the past. But I must say in favor of Focant that he gave a very good assessment of Mark's overt discourse.

*

The covert discourse that is found in Mark's narrative must go back to an eyewitness. Only an eyewitness could have known those things that happened during the life of Jesus and had to be repressed after the resurrection experience. That eyewitness must have been Peter, and Papias must have been correct, when he said that Peter was Mark's source of information.

This information is very important. It changes the way we interpret the Gospel of Mark, and it confirms the theological view that is expressed in the prologue of Luke that what we know about Jesus is based on the disciples' testimony. Luke took for granted that their testimony was reliable. He was mistaken. Their

Other manifestations of the dualism between pre- and post-Pascal

testimony was highly unreliable because their memory of the past was transformed by their faith in the resurrection.

*

Prophets and mystics believe that they are in contact with the other world. Now the other world is the world of the unknown and the unreachable—the world of dreams and visions. That world is associated with the subconscious activity of the mind. The conscious activity of the mind deals with this world. The unconscious activity of the mind deals with the other world. There is here a dualism that is rooted in the human mind. All religions and spiritual insights are rooted in the subconscious dimension of the human mind. Sometimes they take the form of intuitions that we find enlightening and give a meaning to our lives. This is the way in which our mind overcomes the absurdity of the human existence that must end in death. Salvation takes the form of faith in some life after death. The Christian religion is the most radical one. It proclaims that in Christ, death was definitely defeated. This is what a few followers of Jesus proclaimed after their resurrection experience. In the process, however, they had to repress important memories that would have rendered the Easter faith unsustainable, and invent other stories that were pious forgeries. But what they had repressed returned in their discourse and revealed what they had done.

Karl Marx said that religion is the opium of the people. Escape from harsh reality is a form of salvation.

The Christian religion is a testimony to the power of the mind when it acts under the influence of the supernatural.

*

What anticipates the Easter mystery in the pre-Easter context is not historical.

This is my guiding principle.

Part Two—What happened during the life of Jesus.

This is based on the fact that the historical Jesus rejected the notion that he is the Messiah.
My reconstruction of what happened after the second collective meal
and the rebuke of Peter confirm this view.

*

Appendix 1

Note on the Eucharist

*

In his First Letter to the Corinthians, Paul writes,

> ²³I received from the Lord the same thing I passed on to you, that on the night he was handed over, the Lord Jesus took bread ²⁴and after he gave thanks he broke it and said, "This is my body broken for you. Do this to remember me." ²⁵And in the same way he took the wine cup after the meal and said, "This cup is the new covenant ratified by my blood. Whenever you drink this, do it to remember me."
> 1 Corinthians 11:23–25

This text suggests that Paul is the one who introduced the Eucharist as we know it today, and that it did not exist before him. "I received from the Lord what I passed on to you." This knowledge must have been communicated to him in a mystical encounter with the Lord. He does not say when that revelation took place. Most likely this was during his long retreat in Northern Arabia. He spent there some time, in which he had to digest his conversion and rethink his religious views. In other words, he worked out the theological implications of his new religious orientation. This is how he became a great theologian. The other apostles, namely

Peter, did not have a similar intellectual background. Paul became the theoretician of the new religion. In comparison, Peter and the other apostles were illiterate.

But, if Paul had an intellectual advantage over the other disciples, they had over him the historical advantage of having known Jesus during his life. On the other hand, however, Paul seems to minimize that advantage, when he declares that all he needs to know is the crucified Jesus (see 1 Corinthians 2:2).

*

In his letter to the Galatians 1:1, Paul introduces himself as follows,

> Paul, an Apostle (envoy), not appointed by any human authorities nor by any individual but by Jesus, God's Anointed, and by God, Creator and Benefactor, who raised Jesus from among the dead.

This means that Paul draws his Christian knowledge and authority from a divine source. This is made clear when he writes, in the same chapter,

> [11]Let me make it clear, friends, the message I announced does not conform to human expectations. [12]I say this because it was not transmitted to me by anyone nor did anyone teach it to me. Rather, it came to me as an insight from God about Jesus as God's Anointed.

In his special case, Paul did not follow the normal route of being instructed by the church. His knowledge about the Christian mystery comes directly from God through special revelations. Perhaps Paul's spiritual experience can be compared to what Luke tells us about the two Emmaus disciples. Their initiation genius was Jesus himself. Paul seems to make a similar claim. This makes Paul an Apostle like Peter. The only difference between them is that Peter was an eyewitness of what happened during the life of Jesus, not Paul. But, according to Paul, this did not matter, because he received all he needed to know directly from God.

Note on the Eucharist

This claim makes the spiritual and Pentecostal dimension of the Christian religion the primary one. In comparison, what happened during the life of Jesus is secondary. This is why, as far as Paul is concerned, the fact that he did not know Jesus when he was alive does not matter. What matters is that, as the Gospel of John says, he was instructed directly by God (see John 6:45 which quotes the prophets). This is a sign that shows that we are at the end time.

I have no reason to question Paul's sincerity. He must have introduced the Eucharist, and his story must have found its way into a Passion narrative that existed before any gospel was written. Later, Mark could have integrated that Passion narrative in his gospel.

*

Peter found himself marginalized by two very different authorities. First, he was marginalized by James, the younger brother of Jesus, who ruled over the Jerusalem church and continued to believe in the need to observe the Jewish Law. Paul had the audacity and the theological authority to disagree with him. The gentiles who became Christian did not have, according to him, to be circumcised and to observe the Law. Peter was caught up between those two authorities. In Antioch he first followed Paul and had his meals with the converts from paganism. But when James sent his inquisition to Antioch, Peter was afraid of them and stopped eating with the "gentiles." Thus, the early church marginalized Peter in favor of two men who had joined the movement after the death of Jesus and insisted on two different ways of being Christian. Peter was the victim of a double coup d'état, one by James and one by Paul. Eventually the Jewish Christians who followed James will go their independent way. They survived for a while outside the Christian realm of the Byzantine Empire under different names[1]. Paul's

---

1. Muhammad, the Prophet of Islam, must have met some of them in Northern Arabia during his business trips to Southern Syria. That was before he had become a prophet. Those Jewish Christians believed that Jesus was a

views, on the other hand, were destined to become the official views of the Christian world.

*

The four canonical gospels were written by second and even third generation Christians. None of them was an eyewitness of what happened during the life of Jesus. Mark is the only one who had the privilege of meeting with Peter and recording his reminiscences. The other evangelists, including John, knew the text of Mark but took a great deal of liberty with it. They revised, corrected and augmented Mark's short narrative. But their religious message was in substance the same one. This is why they were retained as canonical or authentic (different in form but identical in substance).

I see in the Gospel of Mark the Gospel of Peter. In his reminiscences about what happened during the life of Jesus, Peter was free from James and Paul and their theological disagreements. He remembered the past as best as he could. But he had severe memory problems. I have tried to identify them in the second part of this book.

The Gospel of John is the only one that disagrees with Mark and Paul about the Last Supper. For John, the Eucharist was instituted in Galilee in connection with the sign of the loaves. John must have known Paul's and Mark's texts and disagreed with them. Perhaps the Beloved Disciple had something to do with this, if he was, as we shall see, John's source of inspiration. In this case we would have two different versions of the Eucharist that are based on two different revelations to people who did not know Jesus when he was alive. If this is what happened, how can we account for two different inventions of the Eucharist?

Paul claims that his knowledge was based on a revelation or insight. How could John have had a very similar insight connected to a very different context (the miraculous feeding of the five thousand)?

---

prophet. They did not deify him. The Koran sees in them very close allies (see Koran 5:82–85).

Note on the Eucharist

*

Allow me to speculate

Paul and John speak of eating the flesh of Christ and drinking his blood. This reminds me of a similar ritual that involves the totemic animal. The animal represents the divine. It is sacred and untouchable all year round. But once a year it is sacrificed and eaten in a ceremonial form. There is no cultural connection between Paul and John, on the one hand, and the totemic form of worship, on the other hand. Paul and John must have discovered it independently of any totemic cult and independently of one another. They must have acted under the influence of a deeply unconscious need that exists in the human psyche. I am speaking of the need to sacrifice the god and eat it so that the worshippers may become gods. The idea of our deification exists in the Christian religion. Many Fathers of the Church said that God became man in Jesus Christ so that man can become god. Deep down in our psyche, God must be perceived as the other of Man, and Man as the other of God.

Somehow the Christian religion discovered this deep identity between God and Man. Great mystics like Paul and John seem to have made this special connection between God and Man. Man is in the image of God and God is in the image of Man. God and Man are at the same time different and identical. This suggests that God is produced by our mind, not consciously but unconsciously. Perhaps one can say that the need for a God is built into the depth of our psyche. This is how our psyche is wired. The final result is that, deep down, we create God and, on the surface, God creates us.

The rationalist approach to the gospel that is adopted by academia is inadequate for the study of the way the human spirit works.

*

Appendix 2

The Beloved Disciple

A quick survey

The Beloved Disciple (BD) is mentioned in two distinct sections of the fourth gospel: In the second ending (chapter 21) and in the Passion-Resurrection narrative. In this paper, I will call the author of chapter 21 John Two, and I will refer to the author of the Passion-Resurrection narrative as John One. For some reason that has to be elucidated, John Two says that the BD wrote the gospel. He specifies in the conclusion of his appended story:

> This is the disciple who is testifying to these things and has written them, and we know that his testimony is true.
> John 21:24

In this passage "the disciple who is testifying to these things and has written them" is the BD (see verses 7 and 20). As far as John Two is concerned, the identity of the BD is not problematic. He is the author of the gospel and he was one of the disciples. This means that his testimony is that of an eyewitness who was physically present during the Last Supper (13: 23–25), near the cross (19:25–27) and at the empty tomb (20:3–9). But is this conclusion sustainable?

In this paper, I will argue that John Two's conclusion is based on an interpretation of an ambiguous passage by John One. I will show that the said passage can be interpreted in this way, but that this is an over-simplification of what John One says about the BD.

Most of the time, John One speaks of the BD as if he was a real person and one of the disciples, but one who is never given a proper name. We shall see that the BD is to be identified by his dual relation to Jesus and John One. In relation to Jesus, he is the disciple whom he loved. This privileged situation makes the BD particularly close to Jesus and gives him a special understanding of the Christian mystery. We shall see that he is much more perceptive than Peter in this regard. In relation to John One, he is at the same time distinct from him and identical with him. This is what makes his identity so problematic.

*

In John 1, the BD is explicitly mentioned in three texts:

1—During the last supper:

> [21]After saying this, Jesus was much troubled, and said solemnly, "In truth I tell you that it is one of you who will betray me." [22]The disciples looked at one another, wondering whom he meant. [23]Next to Jesus, in the place on his right hand, was one of his disciples, whom he loved. [24]So Simon Peter made signs to that disciple, and whispered, "Tell me who it is that he means." [25]Being in this position, that disciple leant back on Jesus' shoulder, and asked him, "Who is it, Master?" [26]"It is the one," answered Jesus, "to whom I will give a piece of bread after dipping it in the dish."
> John 13:21–26

Appendix 2

2—At the cross:

[25]Near the cross of Jesus were standing his mother and his mother's sister, as well as Mary the wife of Clopas and Mary of Magdala. [26]When Jesus saw his mother, and the disciple whom he loved, standing near, he said to his mother, "There is your son." [27]Then he said to that disciple, "There is your mother." And from that very hour the disciple took her to live in his house.

John 19:26–27

3—At the empty tomb:

[1]On the first day of the week, early in the morning, while it was still dark, Mary of Magdala went to the tomb, and saw that the stone had been removed. [2]So she came running to Simon Peter, and to that other disciple who was Jesus' friend, and said to them, "They have taken away the Master out of the tomb, and we do not know where they have laid him!" [3]So, Peter started off with that other disciple, and they went to the tomb. [4]The two began running together; but the other disciple ran faster than Peter, and reached the tomb first. [5]Stooping down, he saw the linen wrappings lying there, but did not go in. [6]Presently Simon Peter came following behind him, and went into the tomb; and he looked at the linen wrappings lying there, [7]and the cloth which had been on Jesus' head, not lying with the wrappings, but rolled up on one side, separately. [8]Then the other disciple, who had reached the tomb first, went inside too, and he saw for himself and was convinced. [9]For they did not then understand the scripture which says that Jesus must rise from the dead. [10]The disciples then returned to their companions.

John 20:1–10

There is another passage where an unnamed disciple is mentioned in association with Peter. Some think that this can be the BD.

The Beloved Disciple

> [15]Meanwhile Simon Peter followed Jesus, and so did another disciple. That disciple, being well-known to the high priest, went with Jesus into the high priest's courtyard, [16]while Peter stood outside by the door. Presently the other disciple—the one well-known to the high priest—went out and spoke to the portress, and brought Peter in.
>
> John 18:15-16

In his version of this story, Mark does not mention this unidentified disciple and his role in letting Peter into the high priest's courtyard (see Mark 14:54). This suggests that John created the "other disciple." He must have known that Peter, an unknown Galilean, would not have been allowed into the high priest's courtyard. So, he gave him a helper in the person of the unnamed disciple. In a similar way, he must have thought that Joseph of Arimathea could not have performed the elaborate burial ritual of Jesus single handedly. So, he gave him a helper in the person of Nicodemus (see John 19:39).

This interpretation shows that John One is capable of inventing new details in order to make a story taken from Mark[1] more realistic. But did Jesus have influential followers in Jerusalem, such as Nicodemus, Joseph of Arimathea and the unnamed disciple who helped Peter get into the high priest's courtyard? I have shown that the burial story by Joseph of Arimathea is pious fiction. Most likely, the unnamed disciple is also a fiction. At any rate, he could not have been the BD. All the passages where the BD is mentioned show that he is the BD because he is spiritually close to Jesus, not because he had special connections with the Jewish leadership.

---

1. That John One knew the Gospel of Mark is questionable. It is true that his narrative is in many ways unrelated to Mark and quite independent of his gospel. But John reproduces in his own way many events that are found in Mark and are not historical. This means that either he reinvented them on his own or simply took them from Mark. The last possibility is most likely to be correct.

Appendix 2

In John Two

In the second ending of the gospel (Chapter 21), the BD is mentioned twice, and there is a clear reference to him in the conclusion.

    1 –When Jesus appears at the lake shore, the BD recognizes him.

> [4]Just as day was breaking, Jesus came and stood on the beach; but the disciples did not know that it was he. [5]"My children," he said, "have you anything to eat?" "No," they answered. [6]"Cast your net to the right of the boat," he said, "and you will find fish." So they cast the net, and now they could not haul it in because of the quantity of fish. [7]The disciple whom Jesus loved said to Peter, "It is the Master!" When Simon Peter heard that it was the Master, he fastened his coat around him (for he had taken it off), and threw himself into the sea.
>
> John 21:4–7

    2 –Peter inquires about the fate of the BD.

> [20]Peter turned around, and saw the disciple whom Jesus loved following—the one who at the supper leant back on the Master's shoulder, and asked him who it was who would betray him. [21]Seeing him, Peter said to Jesus, "Master, what about this man?" [22]"If it is my will that he should wait until I come," answered Jesus, "what has that to do with you? Follow me yourself." [23]So the report spread among his followers that that disciple was not to die; yet Jesus did not say that he was not to die, but said "If it is my will that he should wait until I come, what has that to do with you?"
>
> John 21:20–23

    3 –The BD wrote the Gospel.

> [24]It is this disciple who states these things, and who recorded them; and we know that his statement is true.
>
> John 21:24

*

The Beloved Disciple

A crucial text by John One that is ambiguous

As we shall see, the following text is likely to have caused John Two to conflate the BD and the gospel writer into one person.

> [31] It was the Preparation day, and so, to prevent the bodies from remaining on the crosses during the Sabbath (for that Sabbath was a great day), the Jews asked Pilate to have the legs broken and the bodies removed. [32] Accordingly the soldiers came and broke the legs of the first man, and then those of the other who had been crucified with Jesus; [33] but, on coming to him, when they saw that he was already dead, they did not break his legs. [34] One of the soldiers, however, pierced his side with a spear, and blood and water immediately flowed from it. [35] This is the statement of one who actually saw it—and his statement may be relied on, and he knows that he is speaking the truth—and it is given in order that you also may be convinced. [36] For all this happened in fulfillment of the words of scripture—'Not one of its bones will be broken.' [37] And there is another passage which says—'They will look on him whom they pierced.'
> John 19:31–37

In this important text, the one who saw what the soldiers did (verse 35) is not identified. But we can conclude from the context that this unidentified witness must the BD, simply because, in John's narrative, he is the only male disciple who was present near the cross, and could have witnessed what the soldiers had done after Jesus had died. Thus, the connection is made between the BD and the witness whose testimony is considered so valuable by John One:

> He who saw this has testified so that you also may believe. His testimony is true, and he knows that he tells the truth
> John 19:35

As far as John One is concerned, his primary purpose is to bring the reader to believe. He says the same thing in his final words:

Appendix 2

> ³⁰There were many other signs of his mission that Jesus gave in presence of the disciples, which are not recorded in this book; ³¹but these have been recorded so that you may believe that Jesus is the Christ, the Son of God—and that, through your belief in his name, you may have life.
> 20:30–31

This primary concern of the gospel writer explains the importance of the BD's testimony concerning the water and blood that came out of Jesus' side. John One sees in this event a valuable sign that confirms the faith in Jesus.

Let's now examine the testimony of the BD. The first part of the testimony is that the soldiers did not have to break Jesus' legs. I see in this point an integral part of the first burial story, in which the soldiers must have disposed of the three crucified bodies in conformity with what the Jewish leadership had requested from Pilate (see 19:31).

The second testimony is problematic. There is no way of knowing if the piercing of Jesus' side was reported in the first burial story. But one thing is sure: Even if a soldier had pierced Jesus' side with a spear, no blood and water would have come out of the wound. What is reported here is a miraculous event.

John sees in it a sign that confirms the faith in Jesus as Messiah and Son of God. Because this way of thinking is typically Johannine, it could not have been part of the first burial story. As a matter of fact, the main reason why John has reproduced the starting section of the first burial story was that it gave him the opportunity to introduce two cases in which the scriptures were fulfilled, and to exploit the miraculous sign of the blood and water coming out of the pierced side of Jesus. We have here a clear case of Johannine theology at work.

The first burial story has no theological implications. It just tells about the request of the Jewish leadership and its execution by the soldiers. John's interest in it did not concern the burial itself. In what pertains to the burial, he follows the second story that was introduced by Mark and in which Joseph of Arimathea is the main actor. What is noteworthy is that John uses the first burial story for

The Beloved Disciple

theological reasons. It gave him the opportunity to introduce the dual testimony of the BD and subsequently his own theological views.

It is John, the preacher, who addresses the readers and says, "He who saw this has testified so that you also may believe" (verse 35). This means that the BD and John One share the same purpose and the same theological views. What distinguishes them is that the BD acts here as the source of information of John One. Furthermore, the BD is spoken of as if he was an eyewitness of what happened during the life of Jesus. This suggests that important sections of the gospel are based on his testimony. What is even more intriguing is that the text gives the impression that the BD and John One knew each other.

All this raises the question of the relationship between the BD and John One. So far, most of the research was concentrated on the relation of the BD to Jesus. Now we cannot ignore his relation to John One. What is he to the gospel writer? We shall see that he is identical to John One and yet distinct from him. In other words, instead of an "either or," (Kantian logic) we must speak here of "both at the same time" (Freudian logic).[2]

Dual identity of the BD

Our texts speak of the BD in two different ways.

John Two writes,

2. Psychoanalysis and historiography have two different ways of distributing the *space of memory*. They think differently about the relation between past and present. The first one recognizes the one *in* the other, the second one poses the one *next to* the other. Psychoanalysis deals with this relation under the modality of 'imbrication' (the one in the place of the other), of repetition (the one produces the other one under a different form), of equivocation or quid-pro-quo (what is "in the place" of what? There are everywhere masks being exchanged, reversals and ambiguity). Historiography sees this relation under the modality of successive events (the one after the other), of correlation (more or less distant proximity), of effect (the one follows the other) and of disjunction (either this one or the other, but not both of them at the same time). Michel de Certeau, *Heterologies*, translated by Brian Massumi, University of Minnesota Press, eighth printing, 2010, 4.

Appendix 2

> This is the disciple who is testifying to these things and has written them, and we know that his testimony is true.
> John 21:24

Compare this way of speaking with what we find in the following text by John One:

> He who saw this has testified so that you also may believe. His testimony is true, and he knows that he tells the truth.
> John 19:35

Those two texts speak of the BD in very similar ways. Both rely on his testimony and vouch for his reliability. The main difference between them is that, according to John Two, the BD wrote the gospel. But in his text, John One does not mention anything about this point. His message is strictly centered on what happened right after Jesus had died: the soldiers did not have to break his legs and when one of them pierced his side, blood and water came out of the wound. In what pertains to this miraculous outcome, faith is based on the testimony of the unnamed BD. This makes the BD the source of John One—a source that he considered reliable. But what could have made John Two believe that the BD is John One?

Let's compare the way our two texts end.

> John Two: "We know that his testimony is true" (21:24).
> John One: "He knows that he tells the truth" (19:35).
> This is equivalent to saying: "He knows that his testimony is true."

The difference between those two statements becomes visible when we put them side by side:

> We know that his testimony is true (21:24)
> He knows that his testimony is true (19:35)

John Two speaks normally. Speaking for himself and for the Johannine community, he vouches for the reliability of that witness. He says, "We know that his testimony is true." In this statement, we have two distinct pronouns. The first one refers to the subject of the statement "We", and the second pronoun refers to the object of the statement "his". In comparison, John One speaks abnormally. He has the BD vouch for his own reliability. His statement says in substance, "He knows that his testimony is true." This way of speaking is very strange. The subject of the statement "He" and its counterpart, the object of the statement "his" are one and the same. This way of speaking removes all otherness between the subject and the object and makes them one and the same. The consequence is that the otherness between the BD and John One is removed. Therefore one can say that John One speaks here as if he was the BD. John Two must have sensed this point and concluded that the BD wrote the gospel.

In conclusion, I would say that, as far as John One is concerned, he speaks of himself as if he was the BD in one occurrence, not in the three other occurrences.

These are the facts. The question that needs an answer is, "How can we account for this strange situation?"

*

A possible explanation

I will argue in the subsequent part of this paper that what we know about the mystics can be helpful in explaining this unusual situation.

The mystics and their guiding geniuses

Prophet Muhammad believed that, in the mystical experience through which he received the Koranic revelation, God instructed him through the mediation of Archangel Gabriel. In other words, Gabriel was his guiding genius. It is a well-known fact, in the ancient world, that in order to have access to the other world, more specifically to the world of the dead, we need the guidance of someone from that world. This is attested to in the epic story of Gilgamesh. Closer to us we have the literary works of Virgil and

Dante. What is implied here is that we know about the other world through the mediation of revelations made by someone from that world. What is so revealed takes place in the mystical experience. The prophetic experience as it is described in the Bible falls in the same category. It does not matter whether the mystics receive their insight directly from God or through the mediation of a heavenly messenger, as is the case in the infancy gospels. In Matthew's story, Joseph receives his instructions in dreams. In Luke's story, angelic apparitions fulfill that function.

Let me take one more step and ask, "What if the mystic had an ambivalent relation to his spiritual guide? What if, most of the time, he would speak of his guide as being a distinct person, but that on rare occasions he would speak of him as if he was none other than himself?" A seventeenth-century mystic illustrates this ambivalence.

Jean-Joseph Surin

The French Jesuit, Jean-Joseph Surin, tells us about a strange experience that he had during a three-day trip in the company of an illiterate young man. It so happened that they were traveling on the same coach. The illiterate young man revealed to Surin the intricacies of spiritual life. Surin wrote a letter in 1630, in which he tells us about this experience. That letter is reproduced and discussed by Michel de Certeau in his book, *The Mystic Fable*.[3] The road is the symbol of the spiritual journey in which the mystics receive their initiation. The story of the two disciples who were on their way to Emmaus (see Luke 24:13–35) and that of the Ethiopian official who was on his way back home (see Acts 8:26–40), illustrate this point. In the first story, Jesus acted as the initiation genius. In the second story, Philip fulfilled that role. So, most likely, in his famous letter, Surin spoke of his personal initiation into the intricacies of the spiritual journey. The illiterate young man seems to have acted as his initiation genius. Surin refers to him as "my angel."

3. Certeau, *The Mystic Fable*, 207–210.

In one instance, however, Surin betrays himself and puts in the mouth of the illiterate young man something that only himself could have known. Here is what he writes about the young man:

> When I pressed him to tell me whether someone had not taught him after all, he told me no […] Even if the Gospel were to perish, God had taught him enough of it for his salvation."[4]

Compare this to what Ignatius of Loyola, the founder of the Jesuit Order, says about himself in his autobiography:

> "These things which he saw [in his visions] gave him at the time great strength, and were always a striking confirmation of his faith, so much so that he had often thought to himself that if there were no Scriptures to teach us these matters of faith, he was determined to die for them, merely because of what he had seen."[5]

The illiterate young man who was taught directly by God seems to have read the autobiography of Ignatius. In this instance, at least, it is clear that Surin is the one who reproduced an idea that goes back to the founder of the Jesuit Order. He inadvertently put in the mouth of the illiterate young man his own thought. In doing so, he identified with the young man and projected his knowledge on him.

From Surin to John

Based on the similarities that exist between Surin and John, and on the assumption that the gospel writer was a mystic, it becomes possible to say that the BD was to the gospel writer what the illiterate young man was to Surin. The guide is usually perceived as other than the mystic himself. But in some cases the mystics speak as if they identified with him.

---

4. Certeau, *The Mystic Fable*, 209.
5. Certreau, *The Mystic Fable*, 233-234.

Appendix 2

This can be explained by the fact that, in the mystical experience, whatever is revealed to the mystics comes from the otherness of their subconscious.

A similar explanation can be made about the Jesus of Mark who refers to himself as the Son of Man. Originally the Son of Man of Daniel must have been the guiding genius of Jesus. Thus his message concerning the imminence of the Kingdom must have been based on what was revealed to him by the Son of Man. During his life, he must have spoken of the Son of Man in ambivalent terms. After his death, the disciples simply identified him with the Son of Man. This explanation becomes possible if we assume that Jesus was a great mystic (as all prophets are), and that he believed that he was guided by the celestial being of Prophet Daniel.

According to this new interpretation, the BD is the source of inspiration of John One. This can account for the originality of the Fourth Gospel. We have here a mystic who is guided by what he had experienced in his mystical experience. His understanding of the Jesus event is based on his highly personal views, which he believed were imparted to him by the BD.

When we see in the BD the spiritual guide of the gospel writer, that disciple becomes fiction, and he ceases to be a mystery. As long as we assume that he is a real person, as the texts want us to believe, we will have no way of explaining what has taken place in the mind of John One, and subsequently in the mind of John Two.

The spiritual experience is one hundred percent mental. In order to understand what the great mystics tell us about it, we must understand the mental processes that have produced their discourse. This, in turn, can help us to understand how certain components of our sacred books were created.

The Beloved Disciple appears late in John's narrative. But he is present behind the scene from the beginning. The gospel writer relies on him as much as he relies on what was transmitted to him by the community. In other words, the Beloved Disciple and the tradition are the two equally authoritative sources of John One. Thus, his mystical insight is as authoritative as the traditional transmission of the memory of Jesus (Mark). This explains the originality of the Fourth Gospel in relation to the synoptics. His originality is obvious. What is less obvious is his knowledge of Mark.

Some of the liberties that he takes with Mark can be his way of criticizing or correcting him. Here is a good example: According to John, the last supper was not a Passover meal, and Jesus did not institute the Eucharist during that supper.

*

Bibliography

Bird, Michael F., and Sprinkle, Preston M., eds. *Jesus' Resurrection: Fact or Figment?* InterVarsity, 2000.

Certeau, Michel de. *The Mystic Fable*. Translated by Michael B. Smith, the University of Chicago Press, 1992.

———. *Heterologies, Discourse on the Other*, Translated by Brian Massumi, University of Minnesota Press, 1986.

———. *The Writing of History*, translated by Tom Conley, Columbia University Press, 1988.

———. *The Possession at Loudun*, translated by Michael B. Smith, The University of Chicago Press, 2000.

———. *Histoire et Psychanalyse, entre science et fiction*, Gallimard, Paris, 1987.

Codsi, Joseph. "Two Burial Stories in the Gospel of John." The Fourth R, November–December 2018, 17–24.

———. *Enigmatic Texts in the Gospel and the Constitution*. Self-published on Amazon. 2022.

Collins, Adela Yarbro. *Mark, A Commentary*, Fortress, 2007.

Eusebius, *Ecclesiastical History*, 3. 39. https://earlychurchtexts.com/public/eusbius_on_papias.htm

Focant, Camille. *L'évangile selon Mark*, Les Éditions du Cerf, Paris, 2010.

Freud, Sigmund. *Moses and Monotheism,* translated by Katherine Jones (Hogarth Press and the Institute of Psychoanalysis, 1939). A PDF copy of the book is now available on the Internet.

Hansen, Tyler, and Lund, Emily. *Napkin Theology, Small Drawings about Big Ideas*, illustrated by Jodie Londono. Cascade Books, Eugene, Oregon. 2003.

Koran, Chapter 5, my translation.

Lash, Kurt T. *The Lost History of the Ninth Amendment*, Oxford University Press, 2009.

Meissner, W.W., S.J., M.D. *Ignatius of Loyola, the psychology of a saint*, Yale University Press, 1992.

Wrede, William. *The Messianic Secret*, translated by J.C.G. Greig, James Clarke & CO. LTD. Cambridge, 1971.

About the Author

Joseph Codsi was born in Damascus, Syria, in 1933. He grew up in Beirut, Lebanon. He spent 18 years in the Jesuit Order and was ordained priest in 1965. In the second phase of his adult life, he quit the Order and got married. Two Children, Mike and Renée.

The interpretation of some difficult texts from Paul's letters and the gospels continued to interest him. At the same time, he became interested in the prophetic experience of Muhammad. He published a book in which he discussed the two sources of Islam, Judeo-Christian monotheism and Meccan paganism, as they are discussed in the fifth chapter of the Qur'an, *the Meal* (descended from heaven).

The second phase of his adult life is associated with his discovery of America, the new world in which the most advanced technology and the most traditional views coexist – Land of sharp contrasts where the secular and the religious cohabited rather well for a long time. Thus, the new world saw itself as the New Israel and America as the new Promised Land. What is less known is that America is the land of the Law, and that like Israel it needs a Saint

About the Author

Paul to criticize important aspects of the Law, especially when the law is used as an instrument of power.

Codsi is now living in Seattle. He is interested in exchanging ideas, especially the kind of ideas that do not follow the beaten paths.

*

www.ingramcontent.com/pod-product-compliance
Lightning Source LLC
Chambersburg PA
CBHW051102160426
43193CB00010B/1279